Collins *gem*

Stop
Smoking

D1386985

Gill Paul

Gill Paul gave up smoking several dozen times before she finally managed to quit for good. She has tried virtually all of the methods described in this book. When not battling nicotine, she is a writer specialising in health-related topics.

The *Collins Gem Stop Smoking* is not intended to be a substitute for professional medical advice. The reader should always consult their GP regarding any health concerns, particularly any symptoms that may require diagnosis. The aim of this book is simply to offer information that readers may use in conjunction with advice from medical professionals in their quest for health. Should the reader use any information in this book without medical approval, he/she is prescribing him/herself and the author and publisher assume no responsibility.

HarperCollins *Publishers*
Westerhill Road, Bishopbriggs, Glasgow G64 2QT
www.collins.co.uk

Created and produced by
Grapevine Publishing Services, London
Design by Delineate Ltd

First published 2005
© Grapevine Publishing Services Ltd, 2005

ISBN 0–00–719683–0

Printed in Italy by Amadeus S.p.A.

CONTENTS

HOW TO USE THIS BOOK

Stopping smoking – and staying stopped – is a challenge. According to surveys, 70% of smokers in the UK would like to stop but most will try an average of six times before they finally succeed. The good news is that no matter how addicted you think you are, it *can* be done. There are more than 11 million ex-smokers in the UK to prove it, and they can't all have super-human willpower, extraordinary strength of character and nails bitten down to the quick. If you choose the right method for you, it may not even be difficult at all. The aim of this book is to help you to find the easiest way to get free of your nicotine habit, and stay free for the rest of your life.

Every smoker has their own reasons for smoking and their own fears about giving up, so in this book you'll be given the tools to create an individual plan that takes into account your physical and psychological profile, giving you the best chance of success next time you decide to quit. Even if you have smoked 40 a day for the last 40 years, it needn't be a struggle to give up if you find the right method. In fact, it is often harder for the occasional 'social smoker' or one-a-day smoker to let go than it is for a chain-smoker. Nicotine leaves the body completely within a few days, so the physical withdrawal won't take long, but a psychological connection that links cigarettes with 'reward', or 'stress relief' or 'peace and quiet' is harder to break. But don't worry: there are lots of very successful ways to break that mental link.

There are almost as many methods of stopping smoking as there are for losing weight. Like the diet industry, the stop-smoking industry churns out bestselling books, videos and tapes or CDs offering advice and tips; there are umpteen websites, courses, support groups and telephone helplines available to reinforce your decision; your doctor or pharmacist can supply nicotine replacements to help you through the first weeks; and complementary medicine has a wide range of suggestions to ease the process.

However, not all stop-smoking aids will work for everyone. For example, if you only tend to smoke when you are upset or stressed, you don't need nicotine replacement therapies; if the psychological approach offered by stop-smoking gurus like Allen Carr and others appeals to you, they advise that you don't combine it with any other method; and some techniques seem to work better for men than women (and vice versa).

Did you buy this book for yourself or did a well-meaning friend or relative press it into your hands? Even if you're not ready to give up right now, it's still worth reading through the sections, thinking about why you smoke and which methods you would consider when you do try to give up. Plant the seeds in your brain. If you've given up before and then relapsed, try to remember as much as you can about the pressures that made you light up again, so that next time you can avoid them. By choosing methods you've never used before, combined with any that have been helpful in the past, you can give yourself extra ammunition. And if this is your first attempt to quit, choose your plan carefully and you could be one of the lucky 20% who succeed first time.

Part 1 explains how to devise your plan, while Part 2 outlines the main techniques you could choose from. Some of the techniques can be combined while others can't, and you'll find advice on compatibility within the descriptions, along with information on how to find a therapist or group. There are some general principles to help you select the technique that will work for you, but you should make up your own mind about which ones to try based on your self-knowledge and instincts. If one appeals to you, why not give it a go? You've got nothing to lose – except your smoking habit.

Part 3 has advice on how to stay a non-smoker, and what to do if you relapse. Don't ever give up giving up! If you keep trying, using different methods each time, you will get there in the end. It's always better to try and fail than not to try at all. Even if you only manage a day without puffing, you've given your system a mini-break and you've proved that you can do it. And if you've managed a day, you might make two or three days next time and then – finally – the rest of your life.

Good luck!

Devising Your Plan

WHY DO YOU SMOKE?

Tick each of the reasons that applies to you.

• You like the taste... ☐

• Smoking helps you to cope with stress.............. ☐

• You think smoking makes you look attractive
  or sophisticated... ☐

• Smoking helps you to control your weight....... ☐

• Smoking helps you to concentrate..................... ☐

• You get nervous at social occasions and
  smoking gives you something to do with
  your hands, making you feel more relaxed....... ☐

• You couldn't imagine drinking alcohol
  without a cigarette. .... ☐

• Smoking is your reward after a hard day, or a
  difficult meeting, or when you get the kids to
  bed in the evening.. ☐

• Smoking helps you to cope with emotional
  pain... ☐

- Smoking helps relieve boredom............................ ☐

- Life is bad anyway. Nothing good ever
  happens to you. No one cares, so you might
  as well smoke.. ☐

- Cigarettes are your little friend. You've felt a
  huge sense of loss when you've tried to give
  up in the past.. ☐

- You are hooked on nicotine and can't face the
  withdrawal symptoms you get when you try
  to give up... ☐

- Others (insert your own reasons) ....

....

....

Now read on to see why the leaves of the humble
tobacco plant can be so many things to so many
people. How do they do it? (For more on the reasons
you ticked here, see pages 35-43.)

WHAT HAPPENS WHEN YOU SMOKE?

To understand what happens when you give up smoking, it helps to know the way your body reacts when you smoke. Why not light a cigarette and smoke it as you read this section, to identify the physiological responses you can feel? Try and imagine the ones you can't actually sense. It may be easier to distinguish individual sensations if you do this with a first-thing-in-the-morning cigarette, or the first one you've had in a few hours, rather than the next in a chain.

If you are a pipe or cigar smoker, or you prefer chewing tobacco or snuff, the advice in the book still refers to you, but your physical responses will be focused more on the mouth and throat than the lungs.

Ready? Light up now.

Within ten seconds of taking the first drag on a cigarette, pipe or cigar, nicotine droplets are absorbed through the soft tissues of the mouth and throat. Within ten to nineteen seconds, the nicotine begins affecting the brain, causing the release of adrenaline. Adrenaline is a hormone that the body normally releases at times of stress, to put you on high alert –

ready to stand your ground and fight, or to flee from the danger. You produce adrenaline before going in to sit an exam, or if you are approached by a knife-wielding mugger in the street. Within a minute of taking the first drag, adrenaline causes your heart to beat faster. Within ten minutes, the rate can rise by as much as 30%. Can you feel this effect? Some smokers refer to this as 'the buzz'. Adrenaline also narrows the blood vessels in the skin and intestine so that extra blood can reach the muscles, allowing you to run fast if you have to.

Meanwhile, in your lungs, carbon monoxide is replacing oxygen. The red blood cells that normally carry oxygen from the lungs around your bloodstream begin to carry carbon monoxide instead, making you feel dizzy and light-headed. Some people call this 'getting the spins', or 'the dizzies'. When you get this effect, you're suffering from temporary oxygen starvation, which causes your nervous system to go into a mild spasm. You may also feel a slight tingling in your fingers and toes, as they are not getting the oxygen they need.

TIP: Smoking causes 114,000 premature deaths in the UK each year, the majority of them in middle age: about 25% are from lung cancer, 23% from heart disease and 20% from chronic lung disease.

There has been some debate about it, but in 2000 the Royal College of Physicians agreed that nicotine was definitely the addictive element in cigarettes, with effects on the brain that are similar to heroin and cocaine. When you first start smoking, nicotine triggers the release of a feel-good brain chemical called dopamine, and this gives you pleasure. However, after a period, nicotine will actually depress the release of dopamine. Greater and greater quantities of nicotine will be needed to make the smoker feel 'normal' again, and users have the compulsion to keep taking it to avoid the discomfort caused by its absence. Are you actually enjoying the cigarette you are smoking now? Or is it just relieving the withdrawal symptoms you were experiencing before you lit up?

We've seen that nicotine has a stimulant effect, triggering the body's stress response, but in one of the many paradoxes of the chemical, it can also have a sedative effect in larger doses and over time. In fact,

TIP: Smokers like to drink alcohol with a cigarette, so that the alcohol's sedative effects can counterbalance the stimulant effect of the nicotine. Alcohol also numbs the throat so you can't feel the irritant effect of the smoke and are likely to smoke more than normal when drinking.

high doses of nicotine will poison you, causing nausea, vomiting, convulsions, even death. Just 60mg of nicotine on the tongue (a fifth of the weight of an aspirin) would kill a grown man, and young children who eat stray cigarettes left lying round the house suffer severe poisoning. All smokers are familiar with the nausea and jangled nerves after they've smoked too much; these are symptoms of nicotine poisoning.

The heightened physiological responses last for as long as you are smoking and begin to decrease gradually for some hours afterwards, until the nicotine leaves your system or is topped up again. Within one to two hours of smoking their last cigarette, smokers will begin to experience physical symptoms attributable to the absence of nicotine. Their heart rate decreases, they feel anxious and stressed, and they experience cravings for more nicotine, which are relieved when they light the next cigarette. This is why most smokers light up every one to two hours; the average number smoked by British smokers is 14 a day. The relief they feel on lighting up after a period without a cigarette leads many smokers to believe that smoking helps them to deal with stress whereas, in fact, it is the smoking that has caused the stress in the first place by triggering the release of adrenaline, the stress hormone.

If you smoke a cigarette with a filter, you must have noticed the brown tar deposits that form a circle on the white filtration material. Don't let this fool you into thinking the filter has trapped it all. Tar particles are inhaled into your lungs along with the rest of the ingredients of tobacco smoke. The mucosal cells that line your lungs will do their best to repel the invaders, causing you to cough up brown-stained mucus, but plenty still remains behind to coat the lining of the lungs. Over time, these particles are absorbed and cause scarring on the soft tissues.

As lung cells are damaged, they begin to transform into abnormal, cancerous cells, but if you have a strong immune system, your white blood cells will recognise the abnormal cells as 'foreign' and destroy them. The problem is that your immune system is under huge pressure, since it is being turned to 'high alert' every time you smoke a cigarette, and in time it can become overwhelmed. If you suffer from frequent colds, cold sores, or other infections, and it takes you a long time to fight them off, this is a sign that your immune system is overloaded.

TIP: Research suggests that radioactive particles of Polonium-210 are found in tobacco that has been grown in fields fertilised with phosphates, and these will scar lungs as soon as they are absorbed.

WHAT'S IN A CIGARETTE?

Did you think it was just chopped-up tobacco leaves inside a paper tube? Think again. Cigarettes contain up to 600 additives, including:

Fillers

Humectants, which are a kind of moisturiser to prolong shelf life

Sugars to make the smoke seem milder

Flavourings, such as chocolate, honey and vanilla

When these are set on fire, the smoke contains over 4000 chemicals, of which 50 are known to be cancer-forming. They include:

Nicotine	Ammonia
Arsenic	Dimethylnitroamine (causes cancer)
Cyanide	
Benzopyrene (known to cause cancer)	Polonium-210 (radioactive)
Carbon monoxide (the gas in car exhaust fumes)	Formaldehyde

There isn't a part of the body that isn't affected by exposure to tobacco smoke.

• Your stomach lining is attacked by the smoke that you accidentally swallow, which can aggravate ulcers and cause cancers of the digestive system.
• Your liver and kidneys are the body's garbage disposal plants, making them vulnerable to the toxic side products of tobacco smoking. The more poisons they have to sweep up and eliminate from the body, the more likely they are to be affected by them.
• Prolonged smoking will also cause the cardio-vascular system, which pumps blood around your body, to change. Blood vessels constrict, then fatty particles of plaque become trapped in them, physically clogging up the pipework. Your heart has to beat harder to force blood through the narrowed tubes. This contributes to the increased risk of heart attacks and strokes in smokers.

When you think about the massive assault your body is experiencing with every single cigarette you

---

TIP: Smokers who start smoking in their teens have almost double the chance of getting lung cancer as those who started after age twenty.

smoke, it gives you a renewed admiration for the complex design of the human organism. It's quite extraordinary how much abuse it can take – but it's not going to hold out forever.

Every long-term smoker will suffer some kind of illness or chronic damage as a result of smoking. You might be OK so far but, as John Diamond, the author of *C: Because Cowards Get Cancer Too*, who died in 2001 said, every smoker is playing Russian roulette with their health. Which chamber contains the bullet? How lucky do you feel today?

TIP: 84% of lung cancer cases are caused by smoking and 95% of sufferers are dead within five years (most in the first year after diagnosis).

WHAT CAN GO WRONG?

It's not earth-shattering news that smoking is bad for you. Most smokers will skim-read sections of books such as this that deal with health risks, because they don't want to get too scared. 'If your number's up, your number's up,' they say. Or, 'So maybe I'll live a couple of years less but at least I'll enjoy myself in the meantime.'

If it was just a case of you dying at the age of seventy rather than seventy-five, I don't think the government would bother with all those expensive ad campaigns, NHS helplines and prescriptions for nicotine replacements. They'd probably just let you kill yourself. The problem is that smokers die long drawn-out, messy, painful deaths that require countless operations, hospital stays, community nursing visits and medications as they become more and more debilitated. Smokers don't tend to remain active into their eighties, then die peacefully in their sleep. One of the following scenarios is far more likely.

* Did you know that lung cancer is incredibly painful, as tumours eat away at the inside of your chest? In the final weeks, sufferers are hunched over, fighting for every breath, and in such acute pain that ever-increasing doses of morphine can't quell it.

- Have you ever seen an emphysema sufferer trying to climb a few stairs? It's hard for them to exhale; they feel as though they're trying to walk around with a huge, fully-inflated beach ball inside their chest and they're squeezing hard against it to allow even a pitiful amount of oxygen into their lungs.

- Did you know that smoking is by far the biggest cause of amputations in the UK? After the first leg goes, they will fit you with a prosthetic one, but after the second one (usually required about three years later) you'll probably be in a wheelchair.

- Have you ever seen someone with throat cancer breathing through a tracheostomy tube in their throat, pouring liquid food into a stomach port inserted through their skin and writing notes to friends and family on a pad of paper because they can't talk any more?

- Can you imagine living with heart disease and feeling as though there's a time bomb in your chest that could go off at any time? You wake in bed in the morning feeling anxious and your heart begins to beat so rapidly that it feels as though it's about to leap out of your chest, and you don't know whether this is going to be The Big One or not.

Think of the NHS staff hours that are required to look after these people, many of whom take years to die but need regular care in the meantime. They are either taking up a hospital bed, requiring home visits by a nurse, or living in a hospice. All in all, smoking costs UK taxpayers £1.5 billion a year. No wonder the government is so keen for us to stop!

'There's never been cancer in my family,' smokers retort. 'My uncle smoked forty a day and he lived till ninety-five.' 'I exercise regularly and I eat well, so I'm balancing my risk.'

It's amazing the self-justifications smokers can come out with – but they don't add up. Your genetic patterns don't count for much when you are introducing cancer-forming chemicals into your body twenty or more times a day, and three sessions a week at the gym won't get rid of the plaque clogging up your arteries.

The truth is that half of all smokers will die of smoking-related diseases, and the other 50% will suffer some symptoms and illnesses caused by their habit. Want to know what the options are? There's a brief guide on pages 24-5, so take your pick... Except that you can't, because they will pick you.

CANCER WARNING SIGNS

Consult your doctor if you experience any of the following:

Coughing up phlegm with streaks or spots of blood in it

Difficulty swallowing

Persistent hoarseness

Recurrent, severe headaches

Persistent abdominal pain

Blood in urine or faeces, or vaginal bleeding mid-cycle

Change in bowel habits

Rapid weight loss for no obvious reason

Sores that won't heal, moles or blemishes that itch, bleed or grow

Unexplained lumps, especially in breast or testes

TIP: Try taking your pulse before and after lighting a cigarette. How many more beats per minute can you count?

Smokers are at increased risk of:

Agoraphobia

Aneurysm

Angina

Asthma is more severe

Atherosclerosis

Back pain

Brain haemorrhage

Bronchitis

Cataracts

Cervical cancer

Chronic obstructive lung disease

Circulatory disease

Colds are more severe

Crohn's disease (inflamed bowel)

Depression

Diabetes (Type 2)

Duodenal ulcers

Early menopause

Emphysema

Erection problems

Gum disease (causes loss of teeth)

Hearing loss

Heart disease

Heart attacks

Impotence

Immune system works less efficiently

Infertility

Influenza

Intestinal polyps

Kidney and bladder cancers

Leukaemia

Ligament and muscle injuries

Lip, mouth, tongue and throat cancers

Liver cancer

Lung and respiratory cancers

Macular degeneration (causes eyesight loss)

Miscarriage

Neck pain

Optic neuropathy (causes eyesight loss)

Osteoarthritis

Osteoporosis

Pancreatic cancer

Panic attacks

Peripheral vascular disease

Pneumonia

Premature ageing of the skin

Psoriasis

Rheumatoid arthritis

Sperm count reduced

Stomach cancer

Stroke

Tuberculosis

Wounds take longer to heal

TIP: A forty-year-old smoker is likely to have the same facial wrinkles as a sixty-year-old non-smoker. The damage is worst on pale-skinned Caucasians.

SMOKING AND CHILDREN

If you are a smoker, you are harming your children from the moment of conception right through their childhoods, no matter how much care you take to protect them from your second-hand smoke. You are also making it three times as likely that they will smoke when they grow up.

If you are both smokers, you and your partner will find it much more difficult to conceive than non-smokers. *He* will have fewer sperm and those he does have will have low motility (they move more slowly). Even if *she* only smokes one cigarette a day, it is likely to take more menstrual cycles for her to conceive. And at the moment of conception, there could already be problems with the fertilised egg, because the chemicals in smoke can cause chromosomal changes in the sperm, which lead to physical and behavioural abnormalities in the baby. During pregnancy, women are more likely to miscarry, have an ectopic pregnancy, experience heavy bleeding, have an abnormal placenta and, if they carry on smoking after week 8 of the pregnancy, they risk all kinds of health problems for their unborn child.

One in eight women does continue to smoke during pregnancy. It's a shocking statistic. Would you blow smoke into a newborn baby's face as he lay in a cot? If not, how can you contemplate mainlining nicotine into the bloodstream of a foetus in the womb?

If you could watch an intrauterine scan as a mother lit a cigarette and took a drag, ten seconds later you would see the foetus twitching frantically, desperately trying to protect itself from the poisonous cocktail of chemicals rushing into its newly forming cells. The foetus's heart beats about eight times faster while it's absorbing your cigarette smoke.

HELP FOR PREGNANT WOMEN

There's so much pressure on you when you first find out you're pregnant that giving up smoking can seem extra-difficult, if not impossible. There are specific NHS groups to help any woman in this situation; call 0800 169 9169. And don't worry – they will be sympathetic and helpful rather than judgmental.

Here's a short list of what smoking can do to babies:
- There is an increased risk of stillbirth or death within the first few hours of life. Infant deaths in the UK would drop by 10% if all women stopped smoking before week 8 of their pregnancies.
- Babies have a higher chance of being born with a cleft palate.

- They have a greater risk of being premature, which increases the risk of complications like cerebral palsy, mental retardation and behavioural problems.
- There is almost twice the risk that they will have low birth weight, making them much more vulnerable to serious illness in infancy and the toddler years.
- Smoking during pregnancy trebles the risk of cot death. Some experts think that 25% of cot deaths are attributable to smoking parents.
- In the first months of life, babies born to smokers are much more likely to be hospitalised for stomach, breathing and skin problems.
- If a smoker breastfeeds her baby, it is likely to get gastrointestinal upsets from the toxins in her milk, and she will produce less milk than a non-smoker.

Here's what happens as they grow up:
- More than 17,000 under-fives are admitted to hospital in the UK every year as a result of passive smoking.
- Children of smokers aren't as tall as children of non-smokers.
- Children of smokers are more prone to allergies.
- The sons of mothers who smoke in pregnancy are more likely to have antisocial personality disorder, attention deficit disorder, to be aggressive and to play truant.

- Children of mothers who smoke do less well at maths and English. This can be partly – but not entirely – attributed to the fact that smokers tend to be less well-educated than non-smokers.
- Children who are raised in a house where there is cigarette smoke develop far more breathing problems, croup, tonsillitis, ear infections, chest infections and asthma.
- There is some evidence that the children of mothers who smoked during pregnancy will have reproductive problems in later life.

Would you encourage your children to smoke when they grow up? If they see you smoking, chances are they will. Kids are starting ever younger. Did you know that 1% of eleven-year-olds smoke regularly, rising to 22% of fifteen-year-olds, with girls more likely to be regular smokers than boys? A recent American study found that smoking as a teenager causes permanent changes to the lungs, putting them at higher risk of lung cancer even if they stop smoking in future. Teenagers quickly get as addicted to nicotine as adults and experience equally strong withdrawal symptoms when they try to give up. Why would anyone do this to their children? In every other respect, while they might do their best to provide healthy, balanced meals, stimulating leisure activities, warm clothing and emotional security – yet smokers are handing their children a catalogue of serious health problems on a plate.

Most smoking parents will try to protect their children to an extent, by smoking in a different room, or in the garden, or after they've gone to bed. But think for a second about how pervasive the smell of smoke is. You can open a window fully and let a gale blast through a room but it's still possible to tell that someone has been smoking in there. Smoke lingers on hair, in clothes, carpets, curtains and soft furnishings, ready for your children to inhale when they sit next to you on the sofa to watch TV.

There's another dreadful health hazard that children face in smoking households: 44% of house fires in the UK are caused by carelessly discarded cigarettes. It always seems to be the children who are trapped upstairs, engulfed by smoke and flames, while the parents make desperate, futile attempts to save them.

And do you want to die young and leave your children to fend for themselves? Smoking is likely to kill you in your forties or fifties rather than your seventies or eighties. How would your children cope without you?

NOW FOR THE GOOD NEWS

Some of the damage caused by smoking is irreversible – if you have emphysema, you will never run a marathon again – but most of the health risks begin to decrease and your body systems begin to repair themselves from the moment you give up. You will see and feel the differences very, very quickly, and so will your friends. Whatever age you are, it's never too late to start repairing the damage.

By the end of the first day of not smoking, the tar-encrusted cells in your lungs will be under attack. White blood cells will be destroying foreign invaders and tarry mucus will be loosened and brought up as you cough, but this time it won't be replaced by more tar being inhaled. Your red blood cells will carry more oxygen from your lungs, quickly increasing your energy levels and making you feel better. The constricting effects on your blood vessels will lessen and your circulation will improve, so you may find that problems like varicose veins and restless legs clear up. Over time, new cells will replace damaged, abnormal and dying ones and your cancer risk will drop.

If you are one of those smokers who skip all the health warnings and manage not to read the huge black and white messages plastered all over your

WHAT HAPPENS WHEN YOU STOP?

Time since last cigarette	Changes that take place
20 minutes	Blood pressure and pulse return to normal
8 hours	Nicotine and carbon monoxide in blood reduced by half
	Oxygen levels in blood return to normal
24 hours	Carbon monoxide expelled from body
	Lungs start to clear out tar-encrusted mucus
48 hours	All nicotine has been expelled from the body
	Significant improvement in skin pallor
	Ability to taste and smell improves
72 hours	Breathing is easier as bronchial tubes relax
	Energy levels increase
1-2 weeks	Concentration returns to that of a non-smoker

2-12 weeks	Circulation is gradually improving
3-4 weeks	You may feel more cheerful as dopamine release systems get back to normal
3-9 months	Lung function improves by up to 10%
1 year	Risk of heart attack falls to half that of a smoker
5 years	Risk of heart attack is almost as low as someone who has never smoked
10 years	Risk of lung cancer falls to half that of a smoker

cigarette packet, would an appeal to your vanity work? Without fail, smokers look much more attractive within days of giving up. While smoking they have a greyish tinge to their skin caused by lack of oxygen reaching the cells and the smallest blood vessels constricting. Within 48 hours of stopping, their complexion takes on a healthier colour again. Their eyes look brighter and clearer, no longer squinting through a blue-grey irritant haze of smoke. Hair and nail texture will improve over the next few weeks as nutrients are absorbed more efficiently through the digestive system.

As well as looking better, you will feel happier once the immediate withdrawal symptoms are past and your brain's dopamine release mechanism has normalised. You will also feel better because you are doing something for yourself, breaking a negative, self-destructive pattern and looking optimistically to the future. Successful quitters all report increased feelings of self-esteem. You set out to do something worthwhile and you managed it! Make sure you do it for yourself, and not for anyone else.

If you are single, you have a statistically better chance of finding a partner than a non-smoker. That's another reason to be cheerful!

And just think of the money you'll be saving. See the chart on page 75. What would you like to do with it?

All the negative aspects of smoking – stress, anxiety, difficulty concentrating, stale, foul mouth, plus the risk of life-threatening diseases – can be turned around within a matter of days, weeks, months, or in some cases, years of giving up. Isn't it time you started getting some oxygen back into your bloodstream?

ANALYSING YOUR REASONS FOR SMOKING

Let's go back to the reasons you ticked on pages 10-11, look at the false assumptions and the real physical mechanisms behind them, and use them to start formulating your individual giving-up plan.

The reasons why you smoke now could well be different from the reasons why you started in the first place. Did you think it would make you look cool, like a pop star or movie idol? Depending on your age, perhaps you were inspired by Bette Davis, Gary Cooper, James Dean, Elvis, John Lennon, or even Uma Thurman in *Pulp Fiction* or Carrie Bradshaw in 'Sex in the City'. (Note: you'll hardly find any Hollywood stars who smoke nowadays because they're all far too worried about their looks to risk premature ageing.) Maybe you took it up in your teens to appear more grown-up and sophisticated, or to fit in with the rest of your peer group. Some do it to rebel against their parents, while others are just imitating the adult role models around them.

That first cigarette tasted truly horrible. It probably made you cough, retch, or even throw up as the harsh, acrid chemicals scoured your soft, pink respiratory tissues. But you persevered and, by the end of the first pack of ten, you were well and truly hooked, even if you convinced yourself that you were just experimenting to see what it was like.

Everyone knows smoking is bad for you, so you have to find reasons to continue smoking. Which ones apply to you?

You like the taste.

Tobacco on its own is bitter and caustic-tasting, so cigarette manufacturers add ingredients like vanilla, chocolate and honey, some of which are impregnated in the paper. They also add other ingredients to make sure you get your nicotine hit as quickly and powerfully as possible and therefore remain addicted to their product. If taste is the only reason why you smoke, it's time to re-educate your palate and train it to appreciate more subtle flavours. Why not do a cookery or wine-tasting course after you give up?

Smoking helps you to cope with stress.

In fact, smoking creates stress. When you light a cigarette, the relief you feel is just a lessening of the stress caused by withdrawal symptoms from the cigarette you had before this one. Within an hour,

---

TIP: If you manage to stop smoking before middle age, you can avoid 90% of the cancer risk attributable to smoking.

your stress levels will be building again, caused by withdrawal from this cigarette. You are trapped in a vicious circle and there's only one way out – giving up! See page 65 for some ways to cope with stress immediately after you give up.

You think smoking makes you more attractive or sophisticated.

Surely not! Yellow-stained fingers, prematurely wrinkled skin, grey pallor, straw-like hair, milky eyes, those little grooves smokers get on their upper lip, discoloured teeth… is that what you mean by attractive? Why not design your giving-up-smoking plan to include some treatments that will genuinely make you more attractive, such as a hair cut or colour, facial, teeth whitening or a salon tan?

Smoking helps you to control your weight.

Some people use cigarettes to suppress their appetite, and smokers' metabolisms can be artificially speeded up, meaning that they don't absorb nutrients properly. New research indicates that smoking changes the way we lay down fat in the body. Smokers are more likely to have fat bellies, while non-smokers are more prone to laying down fat in their hips and thighs. This is alarming, because cardiac specialists have long been aware that those who carry excess weight in their abdomen are far more likely to have heart attacks than those who carry it lower down.

It's true that you might put on a few pounds when you give up smoking, and if you are worried about this, you should follow the Stop Smoking Nutrition Plan on pages 138-54. You could well be suffering from vitamin and mineral deficiencies, so take a good multivitamin supplement when you give up. And remember that there are plenty of non-smokers out there who keep their weight under control naturally – you don't need cigarettes to do it.

Smoking helps you to concentrate.
On the contrary, smokers' concentration fluctuates wildly according to their current blood nicotine levels. More than an hour or two since the last fag and they'll find it difficult to think of anything except when they can have their next smoke. Non-smokers have much steadier, more consistent levels of concentration rather than erratic peaks and troughs.

TIP: Government statistics indicate that half of British children live in a household where at least one person smokes. In one study, saliva samples from the children of smokers indicated that they were receiving the nicotine equivalent of 80 cigarettes a year.

In the immediate days after quitting smoking, you might find it difficult to concentrate until the nicotine leaves your system. See page 53 for some advice.

You get nervous at social occasions and smoking gives you something to do with your hands, making you feel more relaxed.
First of all, many social events nowadays don't allow you to smoke, so you're going to be extra-jittery at those ones. Secondly, did you ever stop to consider that while you're fumbling with your fag packet and lighter, the non-smokers in a group are watching you with pity? You are dependent on a drug and unable to wean yourself off it, while they are healthy and drug-free. It's not a great first impression to make, is it? If you need something to fiddle with for the first few weeks after giving up, try a piece of jewellery or some cufflinks, a plastic drinking straw, even a set of worry beads. Choose anything that works, and doesn't make you feel too foolish!

You couldn't imagine drinking alcohol without a cigarette.
One of the reasons why alcohol enhances a cigarette is because it anesthetises your throat, so you don't feel the normal irritant effects of the smoke. Smokers tend to smoke much more on nights when they're

out drinking and don't realise the harm they're doing until they wake the next morning with a scratched, raw throat and a mouth like the bottom of a birdcage. When you smoke and drink, you are self-medicating with uppers and downers, constantly trying to find a comfortable balance between the stimulant effects of the nicotine and the depressant effects of the alcohol. You never quite get there, so you keep smoking and drinking more. If this sounds like you, you should avoid alcohol for three or four weeks after you give up smoking; from the sound of it, you may have a problem with your drinking as well (see page 247).

Smoking is your reward after a hard day, or a difficult meeting, or when you get the kids to bed in the evening.
What kind of 'reward' gives you cancer, or heart disease, or circulatory problems that mean you have to have your legs amputated? Imagine you're at an awards ceremony, your name is announced as the winner in a category and you get up on stage, only to be handed a package of life-threatening illnesses. Would you say 'Thank you, I'm honoured to accept'?

TIP: Even if you smoke less than five a day, your risk of heart disease is 2.5 times that of a non-smoker – and the risk is higher for women than for men.

If you find it hard to break the connection between smoking and 'reward', you might try hypnotherapy or behaviour modification to adjust your subconscious thinking. The stop-smoking gurus, such as Allen Carr, all have very powerful arguments to deal with this. And you may decide to find another reward that will work for you, with any luck a healthy one this time.

Smoking helps you to cope with emotional pain.
Many smokers report a dulling of the emotions when they smoke, and sad news will always have them reaching straight for the cigarette pack. As we'll see later, many ex-smokers relapse at funerals – thus hastening their own funeral. The point to understand is that masking pain does not heal it, and leaving it to fester without healing will only make it worse. The healthiest way to survive emotional trauma is to face it head-on, not through the haze of any brain-altering substances. If necessary, get professional help (see page 173). By facing up to difficult situations, you will come through them with increased wisdom and strength that will make any future traumas easier to handle.

Smoking helps relieve boredom.
A cigarette can fill a five-minute wait for a bus, or punctuate the day if you have a boring job, but

maybe smoking is holding you back from making the life changes you need to stop your life being boring. Why not make giving up smoking a springboard to take up a new hobby, change your job, move home, start a family, or find a way to express your creativity? If you're stuck for inspiration, make an appointment with a life coach and see what they suggest.

Life is bad anyway. Nothing good ever happens to you. No one cares, so you might as well smoke. Did you know that depression is a side effect of smoking? By deliberately doing something that harms you, you're reinforcing your low self-esteem. By giving up, and taking better care of yourself, you could turn it all on its head. Higher self-esteem will follow, along with easier breathing and more energy, and the depressant effects of nicotine will begin to clear from your brain. There is something wonderful waiting just around the next corner, but it needs you to take the first step towards it. See page 57 for some tips on dealing with depression when you give up smoking. Don't suffer in silence, or it could get progressively worse.

TIP: Smoking can cause a condition called xanthelasma, in which yellow patches develop round the eyes, especially on the eyelids, due to fatty deposits.

Cigarettes are your little friend. You've felt a huge sense of loss when you've tried to give up in the past.
With friends like these, who needs enemies? Would you keep seeing a friend who consistently made you look and feel bad and was threatening to kill you? Hypnotherapy, behaviour modification or one of the stop-smoking guru books or courses could help you to adjust your thinking. Instead of mourning a loss when you give up, you should rejoice at your success and celebrate all you have gained.

You are hooked on nicotine and can't face the withdrawal symptoms you get when you try to give up.
This is the book for you! You may be a candidate for nicotine replacement therapy, but analyse the symptoms you've experienced in the past and read the advice under each on pages 50-68.

If you had your own reasons for smoking, read on to see which therapies will help you to overcome them. There's an answer for every single one.

TIP: Women who smoke are almost 30% less fertile than non-smokers, and three times more likely to take longer than a year to get pregnant.

YOUR SMOKING DIARY

As you prepare to give up, keep a diary for a week, noting the time and place you had every cigarette and a brief description of how you felt, why you had one then and how enjoyable it was. See the example opposite.

You won't need to do this for longer than a week because smokers are creatures of habit and their smoking tends to fall into predictable patterns. Even if you are not consciously thinking about it for the purposes of keeping a diary, you will tend to light up at exactly the same intervals and in response to the same triggers.

Look at your diary and ask yourself what activities made you want to smoke. Any particular moods that made you more likely to smoke? Which cigarettes were the most enjoyable, and why? Which ones could you have done without, and why? Note the intervals between cigarettes. Were the ones when you hadn't smoked for a while, such as the first one of the day, more enjoyable? Which cigarettes are going to be the hardest to do without? Will any of the substitutes listed on pages 46-8 help?

All the information you learn can help when you are constructing your personal Quitting Plan.

		YOUR SMOKING DIARY		
	Time of cigarette	What were you doing?	How were you feeling?	Enjoyment factor (1-10)
1	09.00	Drinking coffee	Half-awake, groggy	5
2	10.15	Checking e-mails	Annoyed at the amount of spam	3
3	11.20	Making phone calls	Bored, peckish	2
4	12.15	Drafting a letter	Poor concentration, starving	3
5	etc.			
6				
7				
8				
9				
10				
11				
12				

SMOKING SUBSTITUTIONS

First thing in the morning cigarette	Change your morning routine. Squeeze some fresh juices, avoid coffee, have a shower, brush your teeth, do some yoga stretches or 15 minutes of meditation.
Mid-morning or mid-afternoon, feeling peckish or bored	Drink a large glass of water or a small glass of fruit juice. Eat cherries, grapes, or a handful of nuts and seeds. Go for a walk, even if it's just to the local shops or around the office. Call a friend for a gossip.
Feeling stressed cigarette	Choose a breathing exercise from pages 178-82 or try the meditation on page 189. Dot some flower essence on your tongue or sprinkle aromatherapy oils onto a tissue or into a burner. If you can, go for some exercise or try a relaxation therapy.

Needing to concentrate cigarette

Do some deep breathing to get oxygen into your brain. Drink a cup of good, organic coffee. Chew some sugar-free or guarana chewing gum. Dot some flower essence on your tongue.

On the telephone cigarette

Get a notepad and pen and do some creative doodling as you talk. Chew the end of the pen, if you must.

After-lunch energy slump

Avoid heavy, carbohydrate-rich lunches and opt for lighter meals based on fruit and vegetables. Have a power-nap after lunch, or go for a brisk walk round the block. Do some deep breathing and stretches.

Driving home cigarette

Get some great music on the radio and tap out the rhythm on your steering wheel. Chew some chewing gum. Sing!

After-dinner cigarette Clean between your teeth with a toothpick, or give them a brush. Suck a sugar-free mint or have a cup of good espresso. Kiss someone.

With-alcohol cigarette Hold your glass in the hand you used to use for smoking. Twiddle with a plastic drinks straw or a cocktail umbrella. Nibble plain popcorn or unsalted nuts.

Feeling upset cigarette Have a few squares of good chocolate. Call a friend. Hug a pet (or your children). Have a bath with essential oils. Go for a swim in the nearest pool. If necessary, call a stop smoking helpline.

After-sex cigarette Use your imagination!

HANDLING WITHDRAWAL

When you stop absorbing powerful chemicals into your body, there will be a period during which your system is confused and there may be some physical and mental side effects as it adjusts to its new, clean-living, easy-breathing state. It's the same as when you go on a detox diet, and get headaches and bad breath while your body chucks out all the toxins from your liver. The important thing to remember is that these side effects are temporary and will be reversed once you get the poisons out of your system.

There are therapies that can help you deal with every single withdrawal symptom, so there's no need to grit your teeth and suffer in silence. Different people will experience different symptoms, depending on how much they smoke, when they smoke and why they smoke, as well as their individual physical make-up. If you've given up before, you might know what to expect. If this is your first time, use your smoking diary to try and predict the symptoms you might feel. If you've ever been on a long, non-smoking flight, or got stuck for hours in a non-smoking meeting, you'll know what to expect at first.

In the following pages you'll find a list of some of the symptoms you might experience, along with suggestions about the techniques in Part 2 that could help to relieve them. Note that you won't get all of these. In fact, you may be one of the lucky ones who doesn't get any withdrawal symptoms at all.

Anger and Aggression

Within hours of their last cigarette, some people are overwhelmed with feelings of uncontrollable rage. Little things you would normally brush aside become infuriating – the salesman who cold-calls you, the dawdler who blocks your path in the street, the driver who pulls out in front of your car, or the fact that your partner forgot to put the rubbish out for the bin men. These annoyances build up until you are ablaze with sheer fury at the stupidity of everyone else in the world, to the extent that you may even feel physically violent.

If you think this might happen to you, nip it in the bud before you fall out with your friends and family and upset a few strangers into the bargain. Nicotine replacement therapies will prevent aggression from taking hold. There are several effective herbal and homeopathic remedies for anger, and flower essences

---

TIP: For a quick fix for a surge of temper, drink a few drops of oatstraw (see page 128) dissolved in a glass of water.

and aromatherapy can also be useful. Use deep breathing techniques and try to imagine that you are exhaling your fury and bitterness into the air, where it will evaporate.

If you experience unusual anger and aggression when you give up smoking, be aware that it shouldn't last more than four weeks. Perhaps you should warn your loved ones in advance and give them a chance to leave town.

Anxiety

A certain amount of anxiety is appropriate in some situations – for example, when you are sitting your driving test, going for a job interview, or when it's your child's first day at school. However, some people find they are experiencing a constant, pervasive, low-grade anxiety about all kinds of trivial matters immediately after they give up smoking.

Did they remember to lock the door or will they return to find the house burgled? Does their partner still love them? Have they already got a creeping but symptomless cancer spreading around their body?

TIP: Remember that any symptoms you experience when you give up smoking are not a result of giving up. They are all caused by smoking.

There is no need to put up with this kind of debilitating worry, as so many complementary therapies can help to deal with it. Take your pick, from herbalism, homeopathy, hypnotherapy, meditation, breathing techniques, aromatherapy, counselling or flower essences.

Think about the distinction between productive and non-productive worry. By going over a problem in your mind, can you come up with a solution to it? If so, it's productive. If you are worrying about something over which you have no control and that might never happen anyway, that's non-productive. Learn to recognise the difference and when you find yourself engaging in non-productive worry, just stop. Force yourself to think of something completely different. It's easier said than done if you are a worrier by nature, but it's a technique that can be learned with practice. (Behaviour modification techniques can help – see page 165.)

Post-nicotine anxiety shouldn't last more than four weeks. If you are still feeling anxious after this time and nothing else seems to help, you should consider talking to a counsellor to get to the root of your fears. Your GP might be willing to refer you on the NHS if you explain the situation.

Concentration, lack of

In the first one to two weeks after giving up, you might find that you have difficulty concentrating, with your thoughts flitting from one subject to the next. If this is a symptom that has bothered you during previous attempts to quit, choose a date to give up when you don't have any urgent deadlines looming or important projects to complete, so that the pressure is off a little.

If you find yourself staring idly at a computer screen for minutes on end, or reading the same page of a book over and over without grasping the point, there are a few complementary therapies that can help. Try flower essences or aromatherapy for an immediate effect, or homeopathy for longer-term results.

Deep breathing to fill your lungs with oxygen could get your brain back in gear again. Alternatively, you might try chewing a sugar-free gum; all those football managers sitting on the benches use gum to aid concentration while they watch their team's performance on the pitch. Guarana gum, available from health-food shops, is effective.

TIP: Try a few drops of Bach's clematis flower essence to bring your thoughts back to the task in hand (see page 163).

Don't opt for nicotine replacements if this is your only withdrawal symptom, because it will pass fairly quickly and it's not too serious. You may risk people thinking you're a bit flaky when you lose track of the conversation, but before long your nicotine-free brain will work more effectively than it ever did when you were a smoker.

Constipation

Nicotine is a stimulant, and one of the body systems it stimulates is digestion. Many smokers use that first cigarette of the morning, with or without a coffee, to move their bowels at the beginning of the day. When they give up smoking, they may find that their digestion is sluggish for a while – and constipation is not pleasant, leaving you feeling bloated and lethargic, and causing headaches.

Rather than reaching for over-the-counter laxatives, try dietary measures for the first few weeks. Choose wholegrain brown bread, rice and pasta, rather than white. Eat loads of fresh fruit and vegetables; nutritionists recommend five portions a day but see if you can double it to ten. Sprinkle seeds on salads,

---

TIP: Five times more people die of smoking in the UK each year than die in traffic accidents.

yoghurt or muesli – linseeds, pumpkin seeds and fennel seeds are all good. Soak dried prunes, apricots or figs overnight and eat them for breakfast. Drink plenty of water – at least a litre a day – to keep things moving.

If dietary measures alone aren't working, you can buy fibre supplements from health food shops, such as psyllium seeds and husks, isphagula or natural bran. It's important to drink loads of water when you are using these, to bulk them out. Herbal remedies for constipation often contain senna leaf and buckthorn bark as well as fibre, but they are only suitable for occasional use.

> **WARNING**: If you have tried adding extra fibre to your diet and things are still not moving regularly after a month, consult your GP so that other causes can be ruled out.

Cravings

Some people find their cravings for a cigarette manageable, while others do not. If you don't, you should opt for one of the nicotine-replacement therapies and reduce the dosage gradually (see page 96). Acupuncture can help with nicotine cravings, especially if you have some ear pins that you can twiddle in moments of extreme temptation. Herbalism and homeopathy are also useful, and watching the foods you eat can reduce cravings (see page 138).

Cravings are caused by your body crying out for relief from the symptoms of withdrawal from a poison. Remember that if you cave in and top up the poison at any stage, you will only have to go through withdrawal again at a later date. If you can sit it out, you'll find that each craving only lasts for a maximum of three minutes, then it will pass. Find something to do for these three minutes: deep breathing, drinking a glass of mineral water or doing some stretches.

Remember that your brain is playing a trick on you when you get a nicotine craving. It is remembering the sensation when you take that first drag that relieves the withdrawal from the last cigarette. Most cigarettes you smoke aren't like that; they make you feel sick, make your throat hurt and your head ache.

If you have passed the 48-hour mark since you last smoked and the nicotine is out of your system, it would be crazy to reintroduce it now, and you wouldn't even enjoy the cigarette.

TIP: The more cigarettes that are smoked in a household, the more likely that the children who live there will get cancer.

The good news is that cravings soon begin to lessen in frequency and intensity, from several times a day at the beginning to two or three times a day in a few weeks. Ex-smokers report suddenly getting cravings out of the blue, twenty years after they last smoked a cigarette, but by then most can just smile at the memory.

Depression

If you are the kind of smoker who uses cigarettes as an emotional crutch, you might feel a sense of bereavement when you give up, as though you've lost a friend. Maybe you used a cigarette as your reward after a difficult day, or your little secret present to yourself. Of course, in your rational mind you can think 'Some present!' but emotionally you may feel a bit down for a while, as though something's missing in life.

Stopping smoking can also cause depression as the brain's dopamine metabolism readjusts, but this should only last a maximum of four weeks after the last cigarette. There are two easily available ways of stimulating endorphins, the morphine-like brain chemicals we release when we're in love: eating chocolate and doing some exercise. Why not try both? At once?

Most complementary therapies have treatments for when you're feeling low: try herbal or homeopathic remedies, acupuncture, aromatherapy or flower essences, or try a physical therapy like massage or reflexology (see pages 199–200). You might benefit from talking through your sadness, either at a stop smoking clinic or support group, or by seeking help from a counsellor or your GP. All of the stop-smoking gurus deal specifically with this sense of loss when you give up, and show how you can turn it on its head (see pages 87–95).

Don't ignore depression if it persists beyond the immediate weeks after you give up smoking. The longer you leave it untreated, the harder it might be to shift.

Fatigue

You're exhausted, can't stop yawning, and even the simplest chores feel like a huge effort. Your energy levels may fluctuate for a while after you give up, or they may just settle at rock bottom. Either way, be assured that this symptom will pass in a few weeks as your hormones begin to react normally instead of waiting for a nicotine hit to trigger them.

TIP: If you have yellow, discoloured teeth from smoking, why not book an appointment to have them whitened after you give up?

In the meantime, get as much sleep as you can at night, and see if you can master the art of the 'super snooze' during quiet moments in your day. Sit in a comfortable chair where you can lean your head back, close your eyes, and think about relaxing each set of muscles from the crown of your head, down your face, neck and shoulders, chest, abdomen, pelvis, legs, feet. (It may be a good idea to set an alarm clock first if it's the middle of the day and you have other commitments later.)

Avoid rich, heavy meals and opt for nutritious, low-fat dishes with plenty of fruit and vegetables. Make sure any carbohydrates, such as bread and pasta, are wholegrain rather than white, so they provide slow, steady amounts of energy rather than a quick peak followed by a dip (see page 142).

Paradoxically, exercise can help to relieve tiredness; so can herbal and homeopathic remedies, and acupuncture. If your exhaustion doesn't pass after three months of not smoking, see your GP to check there are no other causes.

Fidgeting

Some ex-smokers just don't know what to do with their hands after they give up. Others miss the oral gratification. Lips and fingers are very sensitive areas, with lots of blood vessels and nerve endings, and you might find you miss the physical sensation of holding a cigarette between your fingers, lifting it to your lips and drawing on it.

If you don't have any more serious withdrawal symptoms, don't opt for a nicotine inhaler just to stop you fidgeting. Allow yourself to fidget but find something harmless to do it with, like a plastic straw, or a toothpick or a Biro. You might like to take up knitting or crochet for those idle moments, or learn how to play a musical instrument.

Drink lots of fluids and make sure you get plenty of vitamin C and your fidgeting days should pass (although your fingernails might suffer in the meantime).

Forgetfulness

If your brain feels a bit scrambled and you find that you're doing things like posting your keys in the

---

TIP: Avoid sweets, cakes, biscuits, fizzy drinks and refined, processed foods that give you a blood sugar hit. You may get 5 to 10 minutes when you feel less tired, then your blood sugar will dip again, leaving you more exhausted than before.

letterbox then returning home with the letters, you'll have to slow down and take stock. Before you leave the house, the office, a shop, the car, or anywhere you've been visiting, stop for 10 seconds and think. What did you bring with you and do you still have it? Where are you going next and what will you need when you're there?

Some ex-smokers stand by their front door feeling puzzled, sure that they've forgotten something but unable to remember what. Keys? Yes. Wallet? Yes. What they don't have to remember any more is their cigarettes and lighter, but for a while there will be a nagging sense that something's missing. This will pass in less than four weeks.

Insomnia

Some people experience sleep disturbances for the first one to two weeks after their last cigarette. This is just another symptom of your body systems reverting to normal without the frequent introduction of a powerful stimulant, and you certainly shouldn't rush to your doctor for sleeping pills. There are plenty of other techniques that can help.

Avoid naps during the day or you'll make it harder to re-establish a healthy sleep pattern. Avoid caffeine and alcohol in the evenings, and try to get some exercise every day so that you are physically tired. There are some very effective herbal remedies for insomnia (see Valerian, page 129), and some meditation techniques can help (see page 190).

One tip, which can be very effective when you are tossing and turning in bed, is to hold the insides of your wrists under the cold tap for a couple of minutes to cool them down. You can do this with the inside of your ankles as well, where the blood vessels are close to the surface. Pat with a towel, but don't rub dry. Go back to bed and get into your normal sleeping position, with your wrists folded in to your body. The blood will drain down from your head to warm the areas you have just chilled, and you may find that this makes you sink naturally into sleep.

Irritability

This is a slightly milder version of the anger and aggression some people experience and all the suggestions given on page 50 apply. Try not to get too snappy with your nearest and dearest or they

TIP: If you have trouble getting to sleep, sprinkle lavender oil on a cotton wool pad and place it inside your pillowcase, or buy a lavender-scented pillow. Lavender is a tried and tested soporific.

may go out and buy you a pack of cigarettes just to get some peace. Take a deep breath and empty your lungs completely instead of coming out with that sarcastic retort that's on the tip of your tongue.

Light-headedness
For up to 48 hours after your last cigarette, you may feel dizzy and a bit unreal, partly because you're not used to having so much oxygen in your blood. If this has happened to you in the past, choose a time to quit when you can stay at home for a couple of days without any pressure to perform, and just wait for it to pass. It may be advisable not to drive or operate machinery if the dizziness is intense. Once again, exercise should help.

Over-eating
Eating a chocolate biscuit or a bag of crisps every time you feel like a cigarette is one way to get through nicotine withdrawal – but watch your step. Refined carbohydrates will have the effect of increasing rather than decreasing nicotine cravings and could lead you down the path of temptation.

Read the nutritional advice on pages 138-154 and choose the foods you snack on carefully. If you feel the urge to keep munching your way through withdrawal, you might benefit from reading a book by one of the stop-smoking gurus; they have powerful arguments explaining why substitutions are not a good idea. Hypnosis and acupuncture can also help and perhaps a support group would be useful. Don't opt for nicotine replacements unless over-eating is only one of a number of symptoms you are experiencing and need help to cope with.

When you feel the desire to nibble, try drinking a large glass of water first, because sometimes thirst can masquerade as hunger. If you still feel peckish after the water, consider carefully what will satisfy your hunger, get a small portion of that food and eat it slowly, chewing it well. Try eating six to eight small snacks a day, at regular intervals, rather than having three proper meals, so that your blood sugar levels remain constant. Give yourself a bit of leeway for the first couple of weeks, then start trying to get your eating under control. Keep an eye on your weight and draw a line if you put on more than 4kg (8-9lb). *See also* Weight gain, page 66.

Restlessness
For the first week or so after you give up smoking, you might feel generally out of sorts, unable to settle down, wandering from one activity to another and never

completing tasks. Just be aware that this symptom on its own is not serious and it will pass fairly quickly. Follow the advice under Concentration, Lack of (see page 53) and Fidgeting (see page 59) as required.

Stress

Even when you understand that much of the stress you are feeling is caused by the last cigarettes you smoked, it doesn't help to relieve the immediate symptoms. These can include anxiety, panic, sweating, palpitations, fatigue, irritability, lack of concentration, nausea and a host of other debilitating side effects.

Breathing exercises are the most useful emergency remedy when you're stuck in the middle of an office with a million things to do, feeling wrung-out and panicky. You'll find examples on pages 178-82. A few drops of Rescue Remedy (see page 162) on the tongue can also be invaluable first aid.

To control stress, eat small healthy snacks every couple of hours, and avoid sweets and biscuits that will give you blood sugar highs and lows. Cut back on tea, coffee and alcohol and try calming herb teas like

---

TIP: Rub nicotine-stained fingers with fresh lemon to reduce the discolouration.

chamomile, peppermint and lemon balm. Take a good multivitamin supplement with extra vitamin B and C (see page 148), since these can be depleted during periods of continual stress.

All the complementary therapies have remedies for stress, so try the ones you feel drawn to. Find your own special relaxation technique that you can turn to in shaky moments, whether it's a meditation (see page 189), visualisation (see page 193) or a float in your local flotation tank (see page 200).

The stress of withdrawal from nicotine shouldn't last more than four weeks. If you are still experiencing symptoms after that, it's important to get help because long-term stress can trigger all kinds of serious illness. You may decide to talk to a counsellor to learn some coping techniques.

Weight gain

Here's the bad news: smokers tend to gain an average of 2.5-3kg (6–8lb) in the six months after they give up smoking. But don't forget that weight gain is reversible – chronic lung disease is not.

TIP: Pets in smoking households suffer significantly more illnesses than those who live with non-smokers.

This doesn't mean that you will definitely gain weight when you give up, particularly if you launch into a new exercise programme and eat healthy, non-fattening foods. Some people find that their metabolism slows down for a while without the artificial stimulus of nicotine. This can be part of the reason for weight gain, but the main reason is usually that ex-smokers are eating more. Are you snacking between meals when you used to smoke? Having a biscuit with your coffee instead of a fag? In particular, those who used a cigarette as a punctuation mark at the end of a meal need to watch that without one, they don't carry on to the dessert, then the cheeseboard and the after-dinner mints.

Follow the advice for Overeating on page 63, read the section on Stop Smoking Nutrition and keep loads of low-calorie snacks on hand. Support groups can be useful, as can acupuncture, hypnotherapy, behaviour modification and the stop-smoking gurus.

The main thing is to drop the smoking habit. Once you have got through the other withdrawal symptoms and it seems to be getting a bit easier (after about four weeks), then it's time to start dealing with any weight gain you may have incurred. Don't let it go too far. Calculate your body mass index (BMI) by dividing your weight in kilograms by the square of your height in metres:

Weight (kg) ÷ [height (m) x height (m)] = ?

Check your score:

Less than 15	Emaciated
15–19	Underweight
19–25	Normal
25–30	Overweight
Over 30	Obese

If you have slipped over a BMI of 25, you should start cutting back on your food intake and exercising more. Over 30 and you should get advice from your doctor about a sensible eating plan, because you are at risk of a number of other health problems. Don't ever let weight gain make you revert to smoking, though. You're much safer as a non-smoker with a BMI of 30 than if you smoke and have a BMI of 25. Weight gain is no excuse to start again.

TIP: Have you put on weight even though you're not eating any more? Are you drinking more alcohol? Alcoholic drinks are laden with calories: a bottle of lager has around 145 kcal, a glass of red wine has 119 kcal and a single measure of gin with tonic is around 128 kcal. How many calories did you drink on your last evening out?

PREPARING TO QUIT

Read the descriptions of the techniques in Part 2 that you feel drawn to and work out what arrangements you need to make or products you will have to buy. Still undecided?

• If you think you smoke for mainly physical reasons, i.e. nicotine addiction, opt for nicotine replacement therapies, acupuncture, herbal or homeopathic remedies. Men tend to be more prone to physical addiction so the 'chemical' therapies are more effective.

• If you think you smoke mainly for psychological reasons, such as emotional support or stress relief, try hypnotherapy, behaviour modification or the approach advocated by the stop-smoking gurus. Practise the relaxation and visualisation techniques that appeal as well. Women tend to be more emotionally dependent on cigarettes than men, so the 'thinking' therapies work better.

• If you feel you would benefit from moral support, try a course, such as Allen Carr's or Gillian Riley's (see pages 87 and 92), or join a support group (see page 165).

• The advice on nutrition and breathing will help everyone, while aromatherapy, flower essences and visualisations are optional extras. If you start to experience withdrawal symptoms, check out the herbal advice for your particular problem.

• If you are confident you can manage on your own, read the section on willpower, which will give you a few more tools to use.

• For the best chance of success, combine remedies for your specific physical withdrawal symptoms with some type of approach that addresses your mental addiction.

Once you've chosen your method, the next step is to choose a date. Make it not more than two or three weeks away. If you like, you can select a significant date such as a birthday or anniversary, National No Smoking Day (the second Wednesday in every March), New Year's Day, or the day after you finish your university finals or deliver an important piece of work. If you are giving up smoking because you want to try for a baby, allow four weeks to get the toxins out of your system before you have unprotected sex.

TIP: British smokers claim to smoke an average of 14 a day. 15% light up within five minutes of waking in the morning, and 46% within the first half hour.

GRADUAL CUTTING DOWN

Some people decide to cut down gradually or switch to a lower-tar cigarette, but this rarely works. If you try this, you'll find that you smoke each cigarette more intensively, trying to get the same amount of nicotine into your bloodstream, dragging away at the spent filter to relieve a feeling of deprivation. If you do manage to keep cutting back day by day, you'll just drag out your period of nicotine withdrawal and prolong the misery. Far better to bite the bullet, get through the tricky first days and then take steps to secure your freedom (see Part 3 for tips on staying stopped).

If you are already pregnant, give up before week 8, which is when the fertilised egg starts getting nourishment through the placenta.

If you plan to give up with the help of a herbalist, hypnotherapist, homeopath, behaviour therapist or acupuncturist, make the first appointment your cut-off point and smoke your last cigarette before you go in. Take your cigarettes along to stop-smoking courses and they'll tell you when to smoke the last.

TIP: For non-smokers, kissing a smoker has been likened to licking a used ashtray.

Choose a time when you don't have huge work pressures or any unusual family traumas or upheavals to cope with. If you do a job where you need your concentration to be sharp at all times, you might decide to give up at a weekend or to take a few days off to get through the most severe symptoms. Giving up while on holiday is not such a good idea, because you want to relax and have fun and you could easily let your guard slip. If you give up a few weeks before a holiday, you will enjoy yourself much more once you're there.

Next, you should start collecting everything you will need, such as nicotine lozenges, herbs, vitamins and nutritious foods. Tell friends and those you live with about the date you have chosen so they can offer support (or keep out of your way for the week). Ask them not to smoke around you or leave cigarettes lying around. If you live with a smoker, it's going to be extremely tough, unless you can persuade them to quit as well. If they want to support you, they may agree not to smoke in the house for a while and they should refrain from offering you one in future.

TIP: Some smokers are jealous of those who successfully quit and may try to tempt you. Remember that it's only because you're making them feel bad because they're not as strong as you.

The day before you are going to quit, make sure your fridge is stocked with the right foods and everything you will need is prepared for the morning. You don't have to give up first thing in the morning but if you do, it means you have already been nicotine-free for seven or eight hours while you slept, giving you a headstart.

Don't make a big ceremony of smoking the last cigarette but as you do so, notice how the smoke scratches your throat, how your heart rate speeds up and the acrid taste it leaves in your mouth. Be aware that you are not enjoying it. Stub it out, then wash and clear away all ashtrays in the house. If you have any cigarettes left in the pack, don't just throw them in the bin; break them into pieces and run cold water over them before you throw them out so there's no chance of digging one out next morning. Take a multivitamin before you go to bed.

TIP: People are like circles, and each therapy enters the circle at a different place. If one place is blocked, there's no point hammering away at it. Try another therapy and, if it works, it may open you up to several more.

DAY ONE

When you wake up this morning, you are already a non-smoker, and your life is going to be different from now on. Have a healthy breakfast, take the vitamins and herbs you have opted for, have a shower and wash the stale tobacco smoke out of your hair. If you're not working, you could springclean your home, open windows to air the rooms, buy some fragrant flowers and launder any clothes that smell of smoke.

At some point today, it is a good idea to get some aerobic exercise, such as running, swimming, cycling, tennis or other ball sports. If it makes you sweat, it will flush the nicotine out of your system more quickly. Saunas and steam baths could also be helpful. Best of all, make sure you drink at least 1.5 litres of water (that's twelve large glasses) to help flush toxins through your kidneys and out in your urine.

Attend any stop-smoking appointments you have made. It can help to write a list of all the reasons why you wanted to give up and keep it with you at all times. See the list on pages 76-7 if you are stuck for inspiration.

Decide what you are going to do with the money you save (see opposite). You could put it into a savings account to watch it pile up, or save for a special holiday. Even if you don't save, you'll soon notice that you don't have to take cash out of cash machines so frequently or, if you bought your cigarettes in cartons at the supermarket, you'll notice how much less the bill comes to next time you shop.

Most experts advise that you stay away from alcohol and other smokers for at least the first two days. From Day Three onwards, it will start to get a little easier, although you might still experience some symptoms for a few weeks.

Keep congratulating yourself. It takes a lot of guts to give up, and today is the first day of a healthy new you. You've made a decision to be optimistic about the future instead of self-destructive, and you will soon begin to reap the benefits.

HOW MUCH DID YOU SPEND?				
	5 a day	10 a day	20 a day	30 a day	40 a day
Week	£8.47	£16.94	£33.88	£50.82	£67.76
Month	£36.30	£72.60	£145.20	£217.80	£290.40
Year	£441.65	£883.30	£1766.60	£2649.90	£3533.20

THE TOP TEN REASONS TO STOP SMOKING

1. All smokers are damaging their health and half of them will die of smoking-related diseases. They are not just cutting years off their lifespan but are also likely to have a messy, painful, drawn-out death.

2. Every time you light a cigarette in public, you are showing the world that you are a weak, drug-dependent person. Non-smokers look down on you, and get irritated at breathing your second-hand smoke.

3. Smokers are less attractive to the opposite sex (ask any dating agency) and their sex lives aren't so good because smoking restricts blood flow, affecting the ability to sustain erections and intensity of orgasms.

4. Statistics prove that smokers are much more stressed, depressed and anxious than non-smokers. This is directly attributable to the effects of nicotine.

5. Smoking a pack of cigarettes a day costs £145.20 a month and £1766.60 a year.

TIP: Insurance companies class you as a non-smoker when you have not had a cigarette, cigar or pipe for a year, no matter how much you smoked before then.

6. It's increasingly difficult to find places you can smoke, but smokers' enjoyment of meals, concerts and parties in non-smoking venues is impaired. So they're missing out on a lot of fun.

7. Smokers are not in control of their own lives, because nicotine is in control of them and governing many of the decisions they make.

8. Smokers miss out on many of life's sensual pleasures since their senses of taste and smell are so poor. (Their eyesight and hearing can also be affected.)

9. Smokers' concentration fluctuates wildly, so they will do less well in exams and non-smoking work situations that require intense thought.

10. Smokers smell disgusting. Opening a window, sucking a breath mint and spraying air freshener don't begin to disguise it.

TIP: To get rid of cigarette odours in a room, place a bowl of vinegar in one corner. Cover it with clingfilm and pierce several holes in the top. Your room will soon smell fresh.

HOW MANY CIGARETTES HAVE YOU SMOKED?

Subtract the age when you started smoking from your current age to calculate the number of years you have smoked. Round it to the nearest total shown down the left-hand column of the chart.

How many cigarettes did you smoke per day on average during those years? Follow the column down to where it intersects with the number of years you have smoked to find the figure that tells you roughly how many cigarettes you have smoked in your life so far.

	5/day	10/day	20/day	30/day	40/day
5 years	9,125	18,250	36,500	54,750	73,000
10 years	18,250	36,500	73,000	109,500	146,000
15 years	27,375	54,750	109,500	164,250	219,000
20 years	36,500	73,000	146,000	219,000	292,000
25 years	45,625	91,250	182,500	273,750	365,000
30 years	54,750	109,500	219,000	328,500	438,000
35 years	63,875	127,750	255,500	383,250	511,000
40 years	73,000	146,000	292,000	438,000	584,000
45 years	82,125	164,250	328,500	492,750	657,000
50 years	91,250	182,500	365,000	547,500	730,000

Techniques

WILLPOWER

Perhaps you see yourself as an incredibly strong character. You work hard, play hard, and never make commitments you don't keep. It's a source of pride to you that you have always been able to achieve anything you set your mind to. Now you have resolved to give up smoking and you think you'll just do it on your own, without any help.

You may well manage it – thousands do. What you have to remember is that your brain, the organ you are relying on as a source of cast-iron willpower, is also the organ that is going to be screaming for nicotine. The danger is that the set of nicotine-deprivation signals will over-rule your resolve. It is your brain that will come up with a host of excuses once the withdrawal symptoms set in: 'I've chosen the wrong time to quit because I need to finish this presentation by next week'; 'I'm too stressed to give up at the moment – I'll do it later in the month'; or 'Maybe I should just have one so that I don't feel so grumpy.'

Even the strongest characters have their weak moments, and that's why it's wise to use a method of reinforcing your resolve. Positive incentives work best. Choose from the following, or come up with your own tailor-made ones.

- Get friends and family to sponsor you for charity. Ask them to donate a fixed amount for each week or month that you stay tobacco-free, up to three (or six) months.

- Start putting the cash you would have spent on cigarettes into a separate savings account and decide what you would like to do with it. A holiday in six months? Or would you prefer a treat at the end of each smoke-free month?

- Find a quitting buddy and provide round-the-clock support for each other in weak moments. Helping someone else will strengthen your own resolve (especially if you're the competitive type).

- Set yourself a physical challenge, such as running a marathon, climbing a mountain or doing a parachute jump, and get into training for it. You'll feel your energy levels and physical fitness increase quite dramatically in the first few weeks of training for your goal while nicotine-free.

TIP: Go to a fresh juice bar instead of a smoke-filled coffee bar for your mid-morning break, and go to the gym after work instead of the wine bar.

- If you're single, join a dating agency. When you fill out the questionnaire, tick the box for 'non-smoker' and that way you will meet other non-smokers and hopefully find romance with someone who never knew you as a smoker.

- Go on a course to learn about aromatherapy. Or join a gourmet cookery club, where you need your senses of smell and taste to be in tip-top shape. Or educate your palate about good wines and learn to distinguish your Chablis from your Pouilly Fumé and Merlot from Shiraz.

AVERSION THERAPY

Create your own negative images about smoking and concentrate on them every time a little voice in your head says, 'Wouldn't it be nice to have just a puff?' Some therapists use aversion therapy as part of their treatment process, but your own images can be just as helpful.

- Reread pages 12-19 so that you can visualise all the physiological changes that would occur in your body if you took that one puff: racing heart, adrenaline release, carbon monoxide displacing oxygen in your red blood cells, extremities being oxygen-deprived, lungs filling with tar and cancer-forming radioactive particles. Remember that nicotine is a poison and visualise the toxins coursing through your bloodstream.

• During the last week that you smoke, put all your cigarette butts into a jar of water with a tight-fitting lid. Once you've given up, open the lid and smell the disgusting concoction every time temptation strikes.

• Think of a bedraggled homeless man, searching the floors of the dirtiest public toilets in the town centre for a butt he can light up. Imagine all the stale, dribbled urine on the floor. Think of the germs, the smell. Nicotine addicts can find themselves reduced to some very base levels when they run out of cigarettes.

• Click onto the website www.ash.org.uk. Choose 'facts, stats and pics' from the topic menu on the left, then choose 'images and presentations' and have a scan through the 'smoking and body damage' section. It starts with healthy lungs alongside the lungs of an emphysema sufferer, then shows the differences smoking can make to other organs in the body. The pictures are more dramatic than you might expect. Some images show you the damage wrought by cancer and heart disease. Force yourself to look.

THINK POSITIVE

Every single day, congratulate yourself on your achievement. If you are finding it tougher than you expected, don't be too proud to seek help by trying one of the techniques described in this book. It might be that a herbal tincture bought over-the-counter from the chemist could help you over a particular withdrawal hurdle. Or maybe reading one of Allen Carr's books would underline your motives and help you through the trickier early weeks. Remember: physical withdrawal doesn't last long; you'll be through the worst of it in three days and the remnants within six weeks to three months.

Avoid other smokers for the first few days, if you can, but after that watch people smoking. Notice the addicted way they suck extra hard for the first drag to try and top up their flagging nicotine levels, then watch how they often forget they are smoking thereafter. Think of the brown sticky tar that you see on the filter of a cigarette being inhaled into their lungs. Watch the way they screw up their eyes to avoid the smoke, and the little wrinkles forming as

TIP: Ex-smokers report that chocolate tastes much better after you quit. Now there's an incentive! Why not treat yourself to a square of the most luxurious chocolate two or three times a day?

they purse their lips around the carcinogenic tube. Watch the way they drink more to soothe the irritation in their throats. After you've been a non-smoker for a while, you'll notice how nasty smokers smell when you give them a hug, and you'll flinch to escape the clouds of smoke they exhale.

Look at office workers standing in street doorways desperately gasping on their mid-morning fag. Look at the smokers rushing outside during the interval at a concert, or those lighting up at stations or airports after a no-smoking journey. Smirk to yourself at their frustration when the lighter doesn't spark or matches blow out in the wind. Watch the irritation of other diners in a restaurant when a smoker at a nearby table lights up while they are eating their meal. Remember that feeling of anxiety that smokers get when they're down to their last one or two in the pack, it's eleven o'clock at night and they don't know where they'll find any more. Did you ever cruise round looking for a petrol station at 2am? Most smokers have. They are all slaves to nicotine – and you are not any more.

TIP: Lung cancer has now overtaken breast cancer as the leading cancer killer of UK women; in 1999, it caused 13,110 deaths compared to 13,020 from breast cancer. The rate is still rising.

Rejoice that you are back in control of your life and won't succumb to these addictive behaviours again, but keep your guard up. Remember that if you found it easy to give up, you are more likely to relapse, and the danger could persist for a year or more.

If you slip up and have a cigarette, don't beat yourself up about it. Turn to page 233 for The Emergency Relapse Plan and stop again immediately. Don't lose the impetus you've built up over one little error. You won't be a failure if willpower alone doesn't see you through. You chose the toughest method of all, with the lowest long-term success rate statistically – only one smoker in ten who gives up without using any support will still be not smoking after six months, and only 3% after a year. Why make it harder than it need be? If willpower alone hasn't worked, next time choose some other technique to supplement willpower and resolve that you'll crack it for good.

TIP: Chiropodists can tell instantly if you're a smoker, because you will have dry, rather cold feet, caused by insufficient oxygen reaching them.

THE STOP-SMOKING GURUS

Allen Carr is the best-known of the stop-smoking gurus but there are others, including Neil Casey and Gillian Riley, who have a slightly different angle and extremely useful advice for anyone who wants to give up. All of them use a variety of techniques to help you change the way you think about smoking, and you can 'do their method' by reading a book, listening to a tape or CD, watching a video or attending a course or clinic. There are brief descriptions of their approaches below, but these are no substitute for the real thing. If a method appeals, buy the products or call the numbers given to find out more.

EASY WAY®

Allen Carr's method, known as Easy Way®, claims to remove all desire to smoke so you don't need willpower or any other therapeutic help to quit. He was a 100-a-day smoker for 33 years and had tried to give up several times without success when the idea for the Easy Way® method came to him and he gave up effortlessly on the spot.

His method is a cleverly structured argument that points out that you have been brainwashed into thinking that you enjoy smoking, whereas in reality you don't. No one genuinely wants to be a smoker, and there are no advantages to smoking – none at all. Tobacco tastes foul and makes us jumpy, depressed and anxious, as well as destroying our health. According to Carr, stopping is simple once you understand that you are not making a sacrifice or giving up anything pleasurable. Instead you are taking a positive step towards giving yourself more health, energy and peace of mind.

Carr doesn't hammer on about health risks but drops in the odd shocking fact from time to time. There are some powerful visual images and parts of the argument work on the subconscious level of suggestion. He deals with all the fears smokers have about giving up – how will I cope with bad days? how will I deal with stress? – and shows that after you stop smoking, the good times get better and the bad times are not so bad.

Some of his golden rules of giving up are as follows:
1. Make the decision that you are never going to smoke again. Don't ever allow yourself to question or doubt that decision.

2. Don't use any substitutes for smoking, such as nicotine replacement therapies, over-eating or displacement activities.

3. Celebrate and rejoice that you are a non-smoker. Feel only pity for those who are still trapped in their smoking habits.

4. Don't change your life. You haven't 'given up' anything – you've just cured yourself of a dreadful disease.

Type of Smoker it Suits
Those who are worried about how they will cope emotionally without smoking will find their anxieties soothed by Carr's arguments. His approach could work for heavy smokers who are fed up compromising their health, and also for light smokers who find it easy to give up but are prone to relapses at the first stressful moment. He has a separate book with specific advice for women, and another for those who want to stop their children from taking up smoking.

Effectiveness
Carr's clinics offer free extra follow-ups if you don't manage to stop first time, but only 10% of his clients come back, which could mean that he has a 90% success rate – although there could also be people who don't come back because they felt the method didn't work for them. The clinics offer individual attention and so are most effective, but the books,

tape or video could be useful to keep on hand to refresh your memory if you are tempted to relapse. Revisit them as often as you need to.

Compatibility

Carr argues that withdrawal symptoms are little more than mild anxiety and should just be tolerated for the short time they last, so he advises that you don't combine his method with any other therapies. He is especially opposed to nicotine replacement therapies. As he says, if someone wanted to stop smoking heroin, would you advise them to inject it straight into their veins instead?

CONTACT

To find your nearest clinic, call: 020 8944 7761

E-mail: postmaster@allencarr.demon.co.uk
Website: www.allencarrseasyway.com
Recorded helpline: 0906 604 0220

Books: *Allen Carr's Easy Way to Stop Smoking, The Only Way to Stop Smoking Permanently, Allen Carr's Easy Way for Women to Stop Smoking* and *How to Stop Your Child Smoking.*

Other products: *Allen Carr's Easy Way to Stop Smoking* is available on video, tape and corporate CD-ROM.

THE NICOTINE TRICK

Neil Casey's books and website argue convincingly that smokers have developed a false brain connection making them believe that smoking helps them to deal with anxiety and stress. The first cigarette tastes so foul and hurts their throat so much that they think there's no danger of getting hooked. Then – wham! – by the second cigarette, the nicotine trick is being triggered. It has to be a trick because otherwise, why would any adult in their right mind switch off all their basic human survival instincts and pay money to get lung cancer?

The visual imagery is particularly effective in Casey's books. For example, he compares smoking to an obsessive sexual affair that you know is bad for you and will end disastrously but you can't quite tear yourself away from. He explains how to re-educate your brain to replace any positive associations you've created about smoking with new 'memories'. He even claims that disconnecting the 'crossed wiring' in your brain can help you to avoid withdrawal symptoms when you stop.

Type of Smoker it Suits

Neil Casey's books are shorter and snappier than those of Allen Carr or Gillian Riley and might appeal to a younger audience. He doesn't run courses in the UK (to date) but anyone could benefit from checking out his books, which are an easy but thought-provoking read.

Effectiveness
No data available, but the books are convincing.

Compatibility
Like Carr, he is against substitutes for cigarettes and so doesn't recommend any other therapies are used.

CONTACT

Books: *The Little Book of Not Smoking, The Nicotine Trick*
Website: www.nicotinetrick.com
E-mail: postmaster@nicotinetrick.com

FULL STOP

Gillian Riley runs the acclaimed Full Stop courses, which have a success rate of 75% based on the number of students who are still not smoking a year after attending. Like the other 'gurus', she offers sound common sense that should change your attitude to smoking and she provides a step-by-step approach that you can learn from her books and do on your own, in private.

However, the method is different from the other two as she doesn't instruct that you should decide to give up now for the rest of your life. Instead, every time a craving hits you, pause, recognise what it is and be aware that you have a free choice. You can decide not to smoke right now, and recap all the reasons why you wanted to give up in the first place; or you can decide to smoke, in which case you should be aware that it is not 'just one' but the first of thousands more that you will smoke in your life.

By giving yourself a free choice to smoke, now and in the future, you can avoid the feelings of deprivation that many ex-smokers report. She recommends that you continue to carry a pack round with you and don't tell friends you've given up. If anyone asks why you're not smoking, say something like 'I might have one later.'

Recognise and acknowledge your desire to smoke rather than repressing it. Ex-smokers who repress the desire tend to go round preaching about how disgusting smoking is and fighting a constant battle with their own urges, while those who acknowledge

---

TIP: Smokers produce more of an enzyme that breaks down collagen in the skin, the protein that gives its elasticity.

it will learn how to cope with their desire for a cigarette before long.

Type of Smoker it Suits

Riley's techniques are particularly useful for those who worry about putting on weight, because they show you how to avoid eating and drinking more to mask your desire to smoke. She also runs a programme specifically to help those who have a tendency to over-eat. The psychological trick of letting yourself decide freely whether to smoke or not each time you have a craving could be very effective for those who have felt deprived when they gave up in the past – although carrying a packet of cigarettes around with you could be too tempting for many.

Effectiveness

The courses are 75% effective and the books are definitely worth reading.

Compatibility

According to Riley, substitution is a method of repressing desire that only serves to keep it alive.

TIP: Three out of four children are aware of cigarettes by the age of five, whether their parents smoke or not. Their first instinct is to imitate what they see grown-ups doing.

She recommends that you don't make any changes to your diet or lifestyle in the weeks after you give up smoking. Do exactly what you would have done and eat what you would have eaten when you were a smoker. That means no herbs or homeopathy, and no new exercise regime.

CONTACT

To find your nearest course, send an SAE to Full Stop, PO Box 2484, London N6 5UX

Audiocassette: order your copy from the above address

Books: *How to Stop Smoking and Stay Stopped for Good, Eating Less, Willpower*

TIP: Around 40% of those who have had their larynx removed try smoking soon after surgery, and about 50% of lung cancer patients start smoking again after surgery.

NICOTINE REPLACEMENT THERAPIES

If you go to your GP or pharmacist to ask for help giving up smoking, they are likely to prescribe some form of nicotine replacement therapy (NRT). The idea is that these provide a dose of nicotine so that you can break the habit part of your addiction first without getting physical withdrawal symptoms, then you gradually cut down on the nicotine replacements until you can give them up completely. Past studies have found that someone using NRTs is twice as likely to succeed as a smoker using willpower alone – but more recent research is qualifying this statistic.

> **WARNING:** Consult your doctor before using nicotine replacements if you have heart or circulatory problems, high blood pressure, asthma, thyroid problems, diabetes, liver or kidney problems, gastric ulcers, depression, or if you are pregnant or breastfeeding. Don't ever smoke while using nicotine replacements or you could get dangerously high levels in your blood. Remember that nicotine is a poison.

Nicotine replacements aren't good for you, because they are increasing your heart rate and elevating your adrenaline levels, but they're not as bad as smoking tobacco because they don't have any of the tar or toxic elements of smoke.

NRTs are available in a number of different forms:

• Nicotine patches come in light-, moderate- and heavy-smoker strengths: light for those who smoke less than 10 a day, moderate for those who smoke 10 to 20, and heavy for over 20. Some last for 16 hours, so they don't affect your sleep, while others are 24-hour. The advice is that you use one strength for the first six weeks, then drop to a lower-strength patch for another two to four weeks, then reduce the dose again (if necessary). You should aim to wean yourself off them in around three months, and shouldn't use them for more than five months altogether.

• Nicotine chewing gum is also available in different strengths – generally 2mg or 4mg, depending on whether you are a light or a heavy smoker. You chew a piece of gum until there is a peppery taste in your mouth then you place it between your cheek and your gums, where the nicotine can be absorbed into your bloodstream. Most people start off on 10 to 15 pieces a day; you should never exceed 20 a day. After a month, start reducing the

TIP: About 50% of young adults who smoke just now will still be smoking when they are 60.

number you chew, one by one, and aim to stop using it altogether within three months.

- Nicotine lozenges also come in 2mg and 4mg strengths and, as with the gum, you should keep them in your mouth to let the nicotine be absorbed, rather than chewing or swallowing. Suck one every one to two hours for six weeks, then every two to four hours for three weeks, then every four to eight hours for another three weeks, and aim to stop using them after 12 weeks.

- Nicotine inhalers release nicotine into the mouth and throat, where it can be easily absorbed. Some people like these because you can hold them in your fingers and suck on them in the same way as you do a cigarette, but this can be a disadvantage, since you are not breaking this particular part of your smoking habit. The inhaler can be used up to 16 times a day at the start, then you should begin to cut down after two or three months and aim to stop completely within six months.

- When you use nicotine nasal sprays, the nicotine is absorbed more quickly than with any of the other NRTS. You can have from 8 to 40 squirts a day for the first three months, then start reducing it daily and aim to give up within six months. These are less commonly used, and available on prescription only.

POSSIBLE SIDE EFFECTS OF NRTS	
Patches	Nausea, dizziness, increased heart rate, palpitations, insomnia, headaches, skin irritation or itching at the patch site, cold and flu symptoms
Gum, lozenges and inhaler	Hiccups, sore throat, bad taste in mouth, gum irritations, nausea, increased heart rate, dizziness, swelling of tongue, acid stomach
Nasal spray	Sore throat, coughing, sneezing, irritation of the nose, watering eyes, nasal congestion, cold and flu symptoms

There are a number of downsides to nicotine replacements, and one danger is that you can find yourself hooked on them instead of cigarettes. It's important that you reduce the dose, following the instructions on the pack or the timetable given above, because over the long term they can be harmful. Even with a very gradual reduction in dose, you may experience mild withdrawal symptoms and, if this is the case, you are just prolonging your discomfort instead of getting nicotine out of your system once and for all after three days of complete 'cold turkey'.

Type of Smoker they Suit

Nicotine addicts, who smoke more than a pack a day and know that they have experienced marked withdrawal symptoms in the past, may find that NRTs give them the strength to get through. They could also be helpful for anyone who is afraid of not being able to cope when they give up. They are not suitable for light smokers (less than 10 a day) as they will supply a higher dose of nicotine than you are used to.

Effectiveness

Statistics indicate that NRTs double your chances of giving up long term compared to those who aren't using any therapies at all; around 25% are still cigarette-free after six months, and around 20% after a year. However, a recent study of nicotine gum suggested that it is only effective in the long term when used in conjunction with a psychological therapy, such as attending group meetings. There are also some results suggesting that NRTs, especially patches, are not as effective for women, perhaps because women more often smoke for emotional reasons rather than purely physical ones. If you are a hardened, dyed-in-the-wool smoker, and you think your addiction is more physical than psychological, NRTs can probably help you.

Compatibility

Don't use nicotine replacements with homeopathy, herbalism or acupuncture. Allen Carr and other stop-smoking gurus recommend you don't use them in conjunction with their methods. However, they are complemented by psychological therapies like hypnotherapy, behaviour modification, counselling and group meetings. They can also be used with the Stop Smoking Nutrition Plan, breathing techniques, visualisations and relaxation therapies.

TIP: In 1604, King James VI and I had this to say about smoking: 'A custom loathsome to the eye, hateful to the nose, harmful to the brain, dangerous to the lungs and, in the black, stinking fume thereof, nearest resembling the horrible Stygian smoke of the pit that is bottomless.'

ZYBAN

A few years ago bupropion, more commonly known by its trade name of Zyban, was hailed as the new stop-smoking wonder drug. In fact, it had been used for some time as an antidepressant to treat depression and anxiety and it was only latterly that it was found that it reduced cravings for nicotine. It works by de-sensitising the brain's nicotine receptors while boosting the levels of dopamine, and it helps those who suffer from severe withdrawal symptoms.

Zyban comes in different strengths and is available only with a doctor's prescription for a course that lasts around two months. Unlike nicotine replacement therapies, it is not habit-forming so you won't suffer any withdrawal symptoms when you stop the course. However, you may have trouble persuading your GP to prescribe it since the cost of the drugs is relatively high. He or she may only agree if you have tried and failed using other methods.

Some side effects have been reported, most alarmingly a 1 in 1000 risk of having a seizure (fit), but it is safe for most healthy adults who are not on any other medication. It will not be prescribed to anyone who is already on antidepressant medication, who has epilepsy or eating disorders, or who has a pre-existing mental health complaint such as bi-polar depression. Other side effects that have been reported include nausea, headache and jitteriness, and it is best not to take it near bedtime to avoid insomnia.

Type of Smoker it Suits

Those who have tried and failed with other methods, either because they found the nicotine cravings too hard to handle, or because they became very anxious and depressed, could find that Zyban does the trick for them. It also seems to help those who become overwhelmed with fatigue when they give up. It is advisable to get some psychological support as well, rather than just relying on the drugs.

Effectiveness

In clinical trials Zyban appears to be even more effective than nicotine replacements. A large study in the *New England Journal of Medicine* found that 30% of those who took bupropion were not smoking at the end of a year. However, anecdotal evidence suggests that some users have found it over-stimulating, causing a racing heart, anxiety attacks and manic energy levels.

TIP: Women who smoke have the menopause roughly two years earlier than women who don't.

Compatibility

Tell your doctor about any other treatments you are receiving, whether conventional or complementary, before you take Zyban. Don't mix it with herbal or homeopathic treatments, or acupuncture. Some reports suggest that heavy smokers find it effective to combine Zyban with a few pieces of nicotine gum or lozenges a day, but check with your doctor before trying this.

TIP: If you are worried about taking a prescription anti-depressant, there is a herbal alternative – St John's wort (see page 130). It has similar effects and recent studies have suggested that it can be very effective as an aid to giving up smoking.

ACUPUNCTURE

Acupuncture is an ancient healing therapy that was practised in China over 3500 years ago and is still an important part of Traditional Chinese Medicine (TCM). Practitioners believe that *chi*, a vital energy force, flows around the body along twelve meridians or channels, each of which has around 365 acupuncture points. The harmonious flow of *chi* is essential to maintain good health and keep the balance between the opposite but complementary forces of yin and yang. When there is a blockage, or balance needs to be restored, the acupuncturist inserts fine needles into the appropriate acupuncture points, or applies pressure to them (acupressure).

Acupuncture is extremely effective when used to treat addictions to nicotine, alcohol or drugs. The treatment itself triggers the release of anti-depressant endorphins in the brain and you will leave a session feeling calm, happy and confident. In addition, your therapist might leave three little pins in your ear that you can press or twiddle when you

TIP: You may be able to get a referral to an acupuncturist on the NHS if there are strong health reasons why you need to give up. Several drug and alcohol addiction clinics employ acupuncturists to treat patients, as do some enlightened GP practices.

get a craving, thus reactivating the effects. This is known as auriculotherapy.

What Happens at an Appointment?

When you make an appointment with an acupuncturist to give up smoking, they will probably suggest that you smoke as much as you want up to the time you attend, but be ready to stop then and there. Don't try and cut back gradually.

First of all, the acupuncturist will ask questions about your medical history and any health problems you experience. They will ask to have a look at your tongue, to help them diagnose imbalances. A pink, fleshy tongue is a sign of good health, but if there is a yellow or white coating it means you are below par. Different parts of the tongue correspond to different parts of the body, so they will be able to see where problems lie.

The acupuncturist will then take your pulses, six at each wrist, to check your physical and emotional health. Smokers tend to have a tight, wiry pulse instead of smooth and relaxed. They will probably need treatments for their lungs, liver, circulation and 'earth meridians', covering central areas like the stomach and spleen.

You are then asked to lie down on a treatment bed, uncovering the areas the therapist needs access to, and thin, fine needles are inserted. It doesn't normally hurt, although you may feel a slight sensation, almost like a tiny electric shock, at some points. Some therapists remove the needles straight away, while others will ask you to lie still for around 20 minutes while the *chi* is allowed to flow. After the needles are removed, the acupuncturist will check your pulses again to make sure the treatment has worked.

When you leave the session, you will feel energised, calm, positive and cheerful, no matter what mood you were in when you arrived, and the effects will last for around 10 days. You may find that you cough quite a lot in the days just after a stop-smoking treatment, because the tar and phlegm in your lungs has been loosened.

Your therapist will probably ask you to come back for a second appointment around a week after the first, when you can assess progress and have the pins

---

TIP: . Tell the acupuncturist which side you sleep on so he or she can put the acupuncture pins in the other ear. It hurts a little when you press ear pins, as they are activated, and you don't want to keep waking yourself in the night.

removed from your ear. Thereafter, further treatments will only be necessary if you have other imbalances or health problems to sort out, or if you feel your resolve weakening and want a top-up.

Type of Smoker it Suits

Acupuncture works particularly well for those who are physically addicted to nicotine, and it eases most of the common withdrawal symptoms, such as cravings, anger, depression and anxiety. However, it won't work for those who haven't fully commited themselves to giving up. You have to bring along the willpower and acupuncture will help you to see it through.

Effectiveness

Acupuncture is one of the best therapies for dealing with physical nicotine withdrawal symptoms and getting you through the difficult early days. It will also jump-start your body's repair mechanisms, helping to regulate the blood circulation, the bowels, the lungs, and your brain's natural production of anti-depressant chemicals. Everyone who has acupuncture reports feeling much better after a

---

TIP: In 2002, British American Tobacco, one of the largest companies in the UK, reported an operating profit of £2,681 million.

session – the immediate effects are quite dramatic –
but to stay off smoking long term, you may need a
psychological approach as well.

Compatibility

Combine acupuncture with Stop Smoking Nutrition,
herbal teas, flower essences, breathing and visualisation
exercises, and relaxation therapies to enhance the
effects. It also works well in combination with
hypnotherapy, behaviour modification and support
groups to reinforce your mental resolve. There is
nothing to stop you reading some of the stop-
smoking gurus' books or watching their videos for
some extra ammunition. However, you shouldn't use
homeopathy or Western herbalism in conjunction with
acupuncture, because they may conflict with each
other. Your acupuncturist might prescribe some
Chinese herbs if they are needed to address an
imbalance.

CONTACT

To find an acupuncturist, contact:

The British Acupuncture Council
Tel: 020 8735 0400
Website: www.acupuncture.org.uk

HYPNOTHERAPY

The healing technique of hypnotherapy is completely different from stage hypnosis, where victims are induced to humiliate themselves in front of an audience. Stage hypnotists are adept at weeding out the susceptible types in their audience and putting them into a kind of trance, where they instruct the subject's unconscious mind. This is a dodgy practice which can be severely traumatising for the victim.

Hypnotherapy, on the other hand, speaks to your conscious mind and you remain aware of what's going on throughout the session. You will hear traffic sounds outside, and the therapist's voice in the room; you will know exactly where you are and afterwards you will remember everything that happened. No one knows precisely how it works but physiologically there is a general slowing down of the breathing and heart rate, while your brain is completely engaged with the kind of alert, focused attention you might use when playing sports. In your deeply relaxed state, the messages the therapist suggests to your conscious mind are translated by you into visual images and ideas, thoughts and feelings, creating a kind of link between the conscious and the unconscious. In this way your own imagination backs up your willpower. You can break any positive associations you have with smoking, such as glamorous movie idols in 1940s films, or the 'reward' when you get the kids to bed, or the 'cure' for stress. Hypnotherapy is good at breaking automatic patterns, for people who see smoking as an integral part of their lives and often find a lit cigarette in their hand with only a hazy memory of lighting it. It may be the nudge you need to start seeing yourself as an ex-smoker.

What Happens at an Appointment?

Before you go along for a hypnotherapy session, don't try to cut down on your smoking but be aware of every cigarette you light up. If you are keeping a smoking diary (see page 44), this will help.

Hypnotherapists work in different ways, but they may start by explaining the process to you and finding out if you have any preconceived ideas about how it will work, which could conflict with their methods. For example, they don't swing a gold watch in front of you and ask you to follow it with your eyes! They may then ask about why you smoke and what has stopped you from giving up in the past. The more information you can give, the better, especially if you are a several-times-failed quitter. What is the trigger that keeps starting you again? Hypnotherapy may be able to neutralise this threat.

You will then be taken down into a deeply relaxed state and, if this is your first-ever session, the therapist might use a 'convincer' so that you realise you are not in your 'normal', everyday state of mind. For example, the therapist might ask you to imagine that one of your hands is superglued to the arm of the chair, while there is a deflated balloon under the other hand. He or she will describe the balloon slowly being inflated and you will find that your hand rises up into the air without you consciously moving it. Different therapists use different convincers. It's an important part of the process, to let you know that you are doing something out of the ordinary and accessing a different part of your brain.

The therapist will talk you through some visualis-ations, helping you to see yourself as a non-smoker, and your brain will create its own images and links and store them away. Some therapists use 'aversion therapy', creating associations of smoking as filthy, antisocial, lethal or poisonous. Others will focus on positive associations, such as light, purity, health and

TIP: One ex-smoker described how the hypnotherapist told him that his hands were no longer the hands of a smoker, and after-wards he couldn't reach for a cigarette packet any more. It was as if there was a little barrier in the way.

cleanliness. Different images will work for different people because of the personal connotations.

You will be brought up again slowly and allowed to sit for a few minutes getting your bearings. Many people report a feeling of euphoria after a session. The effects last for about a week, by which time the nicotine will have left your system and you should find it easier to deal with the psychological urges on your own. One appointment is often enough, but you can have follow-ups if there are other issues you want to deal with. If you relapse, go back to your therapist, explain what caused you to slip up, and have another session to turn round the imagery that was at work.

Type of Smoker it Suits

Hypnotherapy won't work if you haven't already decided that you want to give up; it can't make you stop if you are not committed. It is particularly good for those who smoke for psychological reasons, to deal with stress or to anesthetise them from emotional pain. It also helps those who tend to have psychological withdrawal symptoms, such as irritability, anxiety and depression. If you are a heavy nicotine addict, smoking more than 50 a day, you might need some other therapy as well to help with physical withdrawal, such as nicotine replacements, acupuncture or herbal remedies. Anyone can be hypnotised, unless they are psychotic, or under the influence of drugs or alcohol. So long as you find a reputable, qualified therapist, you will definitely find it a positive, helpful experience.

Effectiveness
Hypnotherapy doesn't work for everyone, but it is one of the most effective ways of giving up smoking and other addictions. One study indicated a success rate of 36%, making it even more effective than Zyban. It deals with both physical and psychological withdrawal symptoms in a pincer movement, whereas other therapies focus on one or the other.

Compatibility
Hypnotherapy can be combined with any other therapy described in this book. Allen Carr and an organisation called Quit Masters (see page 170) use elements of hypnotherapy in their courses.

CONTACT
To find a therapist, contact:

National Council for Hypnotherapy
Tel: 0800 9520545
Website: www.hypnotherapists.org.uk

HOMEOPATHY

Homeopathic ideas can be found in the writings of the 5th-century BC Greek doctor Hippocrates, but it was a German, Samuel Hahnemann, who laid out the basic principles in the 18th century. He found that when he dosed himself with quinine, generally known as a cure for malaria, he began to develop malaria-like symptoms even though he didn't have the disease. From there, he developed the premise that a substance that causes symptoms of disease in a well person can be used to treat those symptoms in someone who is ill. It should be no surprise, therefore, to learn that among the homeopathic remedies for giving up smoking are Tobaccum and Nicotinum.

Homeopathic remedies are extremely low concentrations of the substance in question, diluted in alcohol and water. A potency of 2c, for example, is 1 drop of a 1 in 100 dilution added to 99 drops of alcohol and water; for 6c, the same dilution would be done 6 times. Paradoxically, the more dilute the remedy, the stronger the effects.

Homeopathic remedies for individual symptoms can be self-prescribed and bought over the counter in some chemists, or purchased by mail order. However, if you visit a homeopath for a one-to-one consultation you will get a constitutional diagnosis, which takes your entire health, emotional and lifestyle pattern into account rather than simply dealing with one specific issue. Constitutional treatment is a complex art that it takes years of training to perfect, and it can deal with all your physical and psychological problems at once, producing very dramatic effects.

What Happens at an Appointment?

Your first appointment with a homeopath will last between one and two hours, as they ask extensive questions about your medical history, your lifestyle and which inoculations you've been given. The homeopath will ask about any other addictions you or family members might have, and they will ask questions about why you smoke. If there are specific emotional issues affecting you at the time, these will be taken into account.

The homeopath could ask some questions that you might think seem irrelevant, such as whether you are a morning or an evening person, or if you prefer sweet or salty foods. All of these details help them to build up a picture of your physical and emotional type, which they need to choose the best remedies for you as an individual.

For each remedy there is a corresponding 'remedy picture'. For example, the remedy picture for Arsenicum is someone who is anxious, restless, fussy and perfectionist, who fears the night-time and being alone; symptoms include burning pains that feel better when heat is applied, and weakness that seems out of proportion to the illness. The therapist will match your remedy picture as closely as possible to the remedies he or she prescribes.

After the first appointment, you might be asked to come back in two to three weeks, to assess how the treatment is working, and then again after three months, since this is a known danger point when smokers can relapse. Some therapists will also let you call them between appointments if you hit any problems.

When taking a homeopathic remedy, dissolve it under your tongue, without water. Try to avoid touching it with your hands, which could contaminate it. Don't eat, drink, brush your teeth or smoke for at least 20 minutes afterwards, or you

---

TIP: Regular heavy drinking strips the body of B vitamins, while each cigarette you smoke robs your system of 25mg of vitamin C – that's half an orange's worth.

could spoil the effectiveness. (You should have smoked your last cigarette just before your appointment.)

If you are self-prescribing, don't take more than one remedy at once or it will be hard to tell what's working. If you've got the right remedy, you should feel the difference after five or six doses. If you don't, try something else. Don't worry about taking the wrong thing – homeopathic remedies are completely harmless when taken over the short term. If you find a remedy that helps, stop taking it as soon as the symptoms have improved and your own body should kick in and do the rest. One of the main principles of homeopathy is that you should take the least amount of medicine needed to get back on the right track.

Type of Smoker it Suits

Homeopathy can help anyone who truly wants to give up, and it takes a two-pronged physical and emotional approach. It is particularly effective for calming the nerves, quelling irritability and reducing cravings. You might opt for homeopathy if you have other issues going on in your life, such as relationship problems, or chronic digestive complaints, because the therapist can choose a remedy that treats everything at once.

HOMEOPATHIC REMEDIES FOR GIVING UP SMOKING

Remedy	Potency	Dose	Remedy picture
Caladium	12c	1 a day for a week (or longer)	Headaches, sensitive to noise, cravings, nasal congestion, mental anxiety
Staphysagria	200c	3 a day for a week	Anger, indignation, heightened emotion, sense of injustice, suppressed rage
Nux vomica	6c or 15c	2 a day for 3-10 days	Cravings for stimulants, irritability and aggression, sleeplessness, stomach complaints
Tobaccum	6c or 200c	2 a day for several weeks When you feel like a cigarette	Helps the system to detox; will make tobacco taste horrible. Can be alternated with caladium.
Nicotinum	10m	One big dose 3 months after giving up	To knock addiction on the head
Berberis vulgaris	3x, 3c or 6c	3 a day, 3 months after giving up	To tone up liver and kidneys

Effectiveness

Homeopathic consultations should be seen as a partnership between you and the therapist. They will respond to the information you give them, so you need to be fully engaged and committed to trying hard yourself. The remedies can then help to lessen or even avoid most of the common physical and emotional withdrawal symptoms. If you suffer from specific problems, such as anxiety, over-eating or depression, you will be given remedies for these as well. The emotional support provided by a homeopath can be helpful and some can veer into the area of counselling and psychotherapy, if that's what is needed.

Compatibility

Homeopaths ask that you don't use several therapies at once, because it makes it impossible to tell what is working and what's not. It can work hand in hand with some herbal remedies and most flower essences, but mention to your homeopath what you are taking.

TIP: In a US study, it was found that 88% of schizophrenics smoke. Alarmingly, nicotine can interfere with the effectiveness of their medication.

CONTACT

To find a homeopath, contact:

Alliance of Registered Homeopaths
Tel: 08700 736339
Website: www.a-r-h.org

The Society of Homeopaths
Tel: 01604 817890
Website: www.homeopathy-soh.org

For mail order homeopathic remedies, contact:

Helios Homoeopathic Pharmacy
Tel: 01892 536393/537254
Website: www.helios.co.uk

Galens Homeopathic
Tel: 01305 263996

TIP: Why not try Paul McKenna's stop-smoking videos? They can't substitute for the personal, one-on-one attention you will get in a therapy session, but some of the images might be helpful to you.

WESTERN HERBALISM

Herbs have been used since ancient times to treat all manner of ailments. Different traditions grew up in different parts of the world, depending on the basic tenets of their medical beliefs and using the herbs that grew locally. For example, Chinese herbalism aims to balance the energies in each body system, as explained under Acupuncture (see page 105). Chinese herbs wouldn't be prescribed specifically for giving up smoking, but could help to treat any internal imbalances resulting from smoking. Ayurvedic medicine, the system practised in India and Sri Lanka, aims to balance your *doshas*, the three vital energies in the body, and they have particularly effective detoxification programmes. Both Chinese and Ayurvedic herbs should only be taken as prescribed by a qualified herbalist.

Western herbalism aims to strengthen the body systems to help them fight off disease, and when you give up smoking there are some very effective remedies to help your heart, lungs, liver, kidneys and circulation repair themselves, as well as quelling

TIP: If you are a heavy smoker, the oxygen-carrying power of your blood is reduced by 15%, since carbon monoxide binds to red blood cells more readily than oxygen.

withdrawal systems. You can buy many herbal remedies over the counter in pharmacies and health-food shops, or order them by mail order. If you have several symptoms to treat, or if you have any pre-existing health complaints for which you are being treated, then you should consult a qualified herbalist.

> **WARNING:** Herbs can be very powerful drugs. Never exceed the stated dose or take more than one remedy at a time, except under the supervision of a qualified medical herbalist. If you are taking any drugs prescribed by your GP, it is imperative that you take advice from both your GP and your herbalist before you start a course of herbs.

What Happens at a Consultation?

Some Western herbalists are medically trained, so they will do a basic physical check-up, taking your blood pressure and pulse, as well as discussing your diet, lifestyle and any other health problems.

Non-medical herbalists can use a range of diagnostic tools, such as checking the appearance of your eyes and tongue, and the condition of your hair and nails. Some work with crystals, which they can use to determine food allergies and intolerances, among other things.

You should mention any specific anxieties you have about giving up smoking, and the withdrawal symptoms you have experienced in the past, if this is not your first attempt to quit. As well as prescribing herbs, the herbalist might recommend dietary and lifestyle changes, or suggest ways in which you can reduce your stress levels. They are likely to suggest a follow-up appointment within one to two weeks, and more thereafter only if needed.

Type of Smoker it Suits

Herbs will quell virtually every withdrawal symptom, but you have to supply the motivation to give up. They would suit smokers who have been driven back to smoking during previous attempts because of symptoms like irritability, lack of concentration, or difficulty handling stress.

Effectiveness

Herbal remedies are extremely effective. With some, you will feel the difference straight after taking them, although others need to be taken over a longer period to show results. It would be best to combine

---

TIP: For a persistent cough, try Neal's Yard's Clear Lung tea, a blend of expectorant herbs including sage and elderflower. Order it from Neal's Yard Remedies on the number given opposite.

the herbs you need with some kind of psychological therapy, such as behaviour modification therapy, hypnotherapy, stop-smoking guru courses or support groups.

Compatibility

Don't combine herbs with homeopathy, nicotine replacements, acupuncture or any drugs prescribed by your GP, because there could be interactions.

CONTACT

To find a medical herbalist, contact the

National Institute of Medical Herbalists
Tel: 01392 426022
Website: www.nimh.org.uk

For mail order herbal remedies, contact:

Neals' Yard Remedies
Tel. 0845 2623145

Victoria Health
Tel: 0800 413596

The Nutri Centre
Tel: 0800 587 2290

Napiers
Tel: 0131 343 6683

SELF-PRESCRIBING HERBS

In the following pages, you will find twelve common herbal remedies that could help you to quit smoking. Choose the one that is indicated for the symptoms you are experiencing and follow the recommended dosage. Read all the contraindications on the packaging and remember to check with your GP if you are taking any other medications or have a pre-existing health complaint.

• You can buy herbs as a tincture, which is the herbal extract soaked in an alcohol base. You then dissolve a few drops in a glass of water and drink it.

• Solid extracts are the dried and powdered herbs formed into tablets or capsules. Follow the instructions if you are asked to take them with food, or with liquid.

Always buy remedies that are standardised, if possible, so you can be sure of the dose you are receiving in each tablet. Non-standardised preparations might be cheaper, but they often contain hardly any of the active ingredient.

HERBAL REMEDIES AND SUPPLEMENTS FOR GIVING UP SMOKING

Symptoms	Remedies that can help
Anger, irritability, cravings	Oatstraw (see page 128)
Insomnia, anxiety, stress	Valerian combinations (see page 129)
Cravings, congested lungs	Lobelia (see page 130)
Depression, anxiety	St John's wort (see page 130)
Depression, over-eating	L-Phenylalanine (see page 131)
Poor concentration, bad circulation	Gingko biloba (see page 132)
Stress, weakened immune system	Astralagus (see page 133)
Stress, digestive problems	Liquorice root (see page 134)
Poor circulation, furring of arteries	Pine bark (see page 135)
Coughing, tightness in the lungs	N-acetyl cysteine (see page 135)
Impaired immune system	Goldenseal (see page 136)
Mental cloudiness, energy dips	Ginseng (see page 136)

Oatstraw (*Avena sativa*)

The number one stop-smoking supplement, raved about by all who try it, is oatstraw (*Avena sativa*), otherwise known as wild oats. It is sold as a brown tincture and you dissolve a dropperful in a glass of water then drink it. Take it two or three times a day when nicotine cravings are at their worst and you'll find it quells them instantly, or try some when you feel stressed for an immediate sense of calm and serenity.

Oatstraw is full of B group vitamins, which act on the nervous system to relieve depression, exhaustion and stress. It is also packed full of flavonoids, a kind of steroid, and loads of minerals, especially calcium.

It's a good idea for all quitters to have this on hand for the first few weeks, and take it at those moments when you feel ready to kill the next person who walks into the room! Carry a bottle around with you and make it a rule that you will take a dose whenever you are tempted to have that relapse cigarette. It could make all the difference.

TIP: As well as relieving stress and grumpiness, oatstraw can help to reduce high cholesterol levels and will also ease another common nicotine withdrawal side effect – constipation.

Valerian

A wonderfully calming herb that will relieve daytime stress and anxiety, and ensure a good night's sleep as well. It contains chemicals that ease over-stimulation of the brain and it also works as a muscle relaxant that can relieve cramp, rheumatic pains and irritable bowel syndrome.

Unlike prescription sleeping pills, valerian shouldn't leave you feeling groggy and hungover the next morning. It is often sold in combination with other soothing herbs, such as hops or lemon balm. An effective formulation called Aim Calm, containing valerian, vervain, skullcap and hops, is available from Napier's (see page 125).

> **WARNING:** Don't take valerian if you are pregnant or breastfeeding, or if you are taking any other sleeping pills. It may cause drowsiness, which could be dangerous if you are driving or operating machinery.

Follow the instructions on the product you buy. For valerian on its own, you will probably be instructed to take 250-800mg two or three times a day. If you are just using it to sleep, take one or two 450mg capsules an hour before you go to bed. If you buy valerian as a tincture (available from Neal's Yard), you can dissolve ten drops in a glass of water and drink it at any time of day to relieve anxiety and panicky feelings.

Lobelia

Lobelia is very effective at reducing nicotine cravings, because it lodges in the same brain receptor sites as nicotine. It is also good for loosening and clearing out tar and phlegm from the lungs, and will calm the worst ravages of a hacking smoker's cough.

Lobelia can cause nausea in large doses, so one of the most effective ways to take it is in the form of a cough syrup. There is a good one available from Napier's (see page 125). Take a 5ml spoonful three or four times daily, as required.

St John's wort (Hypericum)

The petals of this yellow flower contain a powerful antidepressant that works by prolonging the action of the brain chemical serotonin, and reducing the level of stress hormones. It takes two to three weeks before it starts to work, so if you have been prone to depression and anxiety during previous attempts to quit you may wish to begin taking it before you give up.

This is one of the best-known herbal remedies and dozens of clinical tests have proved its efficacy in treating mild to moderate depression. In one study, 75% of a group of 5000 subjects showed a significant improvement after five weeks, and 33% were completely depression free. Recent studies have indicated it can be very effective as a stop-smoking tool, in the same way as Zyban (see page 102).

Take a 300mg tablet three times a day, or buy the one-a-day formulations. They're available in most chemists, and even in some supermarkets. Take them with food, and avoid drinking alcohol. There is a long list of drugs that should not be taken at the same time as St Johns' wort, but on its own it is perfectly safe and very useful.

> **WARNING:** Check with your doctor if you are on any prescription medications, as it could interfere with their action. It may stop the contraceptive pill from working, so beware! There is also a chance that St John's wort can cause photosensitivity if you are taking certain medications and are fair-skinned. It should not be taken if you are pregnant or breastfeeding.

L-Phenylalanine

This is an essential amino acid, not a herb, and it is involved in the production of dopamine and noradrenaline, as well as several other brain chemicals. Taking supplements of phenylalanine when you give up smoking can help to ease depression and make you feel more mentally alert. It also quells appetite and, as an added bonus, you may find it boosts your sex drive.

Take between 500mg and 1g a day for three weeks, or buy a supplement called Nico-Quit, which is available from the Nutri Centre (see page 125). Cut down on the dose if you find it is over-stimulating you or causing sleep disturbance or anxiety.

> **WARNING**: Avoid taking L-Phenylalanine if you have high blood pressure, malignant melanoma, phenylketonuria, or if you are already taking an anti-depressant.

Gingko biloba

This is one of the most popular herbal supplements in Europe, taken to boost memory and concentration and improve the circulation, thus easing conditions like varicose veins, restless legs and dizziness on standing up. It can also help ease depression and anxiety, and it's particularly useful for men who have difficulty achieving or maintaining erections.

The leaves of the gingko plant contain a host of powerful antioxidants, bioflavones, and chemicals known as ginkgolides and bilobalides, which relax blood vessels and prevent platelet cells from clumping together. Studies show that within one hour of taking it, the blood flow to capillaries in the fingernails is increased, but the full benefits may not be noticeable for 10 days to 12 weeks after you start taking it.

You should take at least 120mg a day, either as two or three 40-60mg tablets, or as a one-a-day formulation.

> **WARNING:** Not for use by anyone taking blood-thinning drugs, or aspirin.

Astralagus

Astralagus is a heavyweight in the world of herbs, working on many different systems to help the body cope with stress, to improve mood and to boost the immune system. It increases the production of red blood cells to help the circulation of oxygen round the body, and can help to break down plaque in the blood vessels that could cause heart attacks and strokes. Meanwhile, it stimulates white blood cells to

---

TIP: Do you ever find yourself saying: 'Smoking doesn't affect me. I just suffer from hay fever/catarrh/dust allergy and that's why I'm coughing'? Smokers have many ways of deluding themselves.

destroy foreign invaders and protects the liver and kidneys, among many other functions.

Astralagus should not be taken long term. When giving up smoking, take 400mg a day for a month, then cut back to 200mg for another month.

> **WARNING**: Avoid taking if you have a fever, suffer from skin problems, or if you are pregnant or breastfeeding.

Liquorice root

Chewing a piece of liquorice root or sucking a liquorice lozenge is a great way of dealing with nicotine cravings, and has many other beneficial effects. Extracts containing glycyrrhizin are good for combatting stress and relieving digestive symptoms like bloating and flatulence, and they will thin phlegm, making it easier to cough up the tar from your lungs.

If you are using cut or powdered root, don't exceed 15g a day. Don't take liquorice for more than a month, and avoid it if you have high blood pressure, liver or kidney problems, or if you are pregnant. Note that it is

TIP: If you stop smoking at 50, you will half your risk of dying within the next 15 years compared to those who are still smoking.

also quite an effective laxative, so you may need to cut back if it is working too efficiently in this way.

Pine bark (Pycnogenol)

Pine bark extracts are great for the circulation and may help to break up deposits of plaque in the arteries and reduce the clotting that can cause heart attacks and strokes. It is also a powerful antioxidant and can help to prevent cancer. If you have symptoms of poor circulation, such as varicose veins, restless legs or impotence, it can be a good idea to take pycnogenol after you give up smoking to help your arteries begin to repair themselves. The recommended dose is between 50 and 200mg a day.

N-acetyl cysteine

This is not a herb, but an amino acid that boosts the production of an antioxidant called glutathione, which works on the respiratory system. It helps to loosen up mucus, which will shift tarry deposits from your lungs, and some research studies indicate that it can prevent some of the cellular damage that causes lung cancer.

TIP: Take 125mg pycnogenol before a long-distance flight to prevent economy-class syndrome, or deep vein thrombosis. It is as effective as aspirin, but without the risk of irritating the stomach lining.

Take up to 500mg three times a day if you are coughing a lot and your lungs feel tight when you give up. Avoid this supplement if you suffer from peptic ulcers.

Goldenseal

Goldenseal is great for helping to cleanse foreign substances from the body and boosting the immune system. It is antibacterial and antiviral, and it increases the flow of blood to the spleen, where foreign bodies are filtered out.

It is often taken at the same time as echinacea, another well-known immune system booster; try taking one for two weeks then switching to the other. When giving up smoking, you can take 125mg goldenseal two to four times daily for two weeks, to give the body's healing mechanisms a jump start.

> **WARNING:** Don't take if you have high blood pressure, glaucoma, or if you are pregnant or breastfeeding.

Ginseng (*P. quinquefolium, P. ginseng*)

American ginseng (*P. quinquefolium*) is calming and good for treating anxiety and insomnia, while the Korean kind (*P. ginseng*) is stimulating and better for fatigue. Both types help you to deal with stress and will improve mental alertness and energy levels. Research trials have shown that those taking ginseng have faster reaction times than others in a control group.

Ginseng also has a restorative action on the body, improving lung function and circulation, helping the cells to take up oxygen and increasing the release of sex hormones.

Choose a standardised product with at least 5% ginsenosides and take around 600mg daily for six weeks.

> **WARNING:** Don't take ginseng if you have high blood pressure or any heart problems, or if you are pregnant or have cancer.

TIP: For advice on multivitamins and minerals that you should take when you give up smoking, see pages 148-51.

THE STOP SMOKING NUTRITION PLAN

Nutrition can be helpful in many ways when you are giving up smoking. You can take vitamin and mineral supplements and eat foods that encourage your body to start repairing the damage caused by smoking, and you can also opt for foods that will help to reduce nicotine cravings, and give you extra energy. There are five simple rules in this section, which will make your quitting experience easier and make you feel healthier very quickly.

1. OPT FOR AN ALKALINE BALANCE

Try eating an apple. You don't feel like a cigarette immediately afterwards, do you? But a doughnut and a cup of coffee will have you reaching for the packet immediately. This reaction may be partly due to the association you have in your mind (cup of coffee + doughnut = time for a ciggie), but there is another reason too. Foods and drinks that have an overall acid-forming effect after digestion by the body increase cravings for nicotine and those with an alkaline-forming effect decrease them.

Cast your mind back to those school chemistry lessons. All substances have a pH number of 1 to 14, where 7 is neutral, less than 7 is acid and more than 7 is alkaline. If you add an acid and an alkali together, they will neutralize each other. That's really all the science you need to understand. The trick when giving up smoking is to focus on foods that have an alkaline-forming residue – but they may not be the foods you think.

- Most proteins – fish, meat and eggs – are acid-forming
- Milk, Gruyère cheese and Parmesan are alkaline-forming
- Breads, pasta, rice and cereals tend to be acid-forming
- Most fruits and vegetables are alkaline-forming

By great good chance, the foods that decrease cravings for nicotine are also ones that tend to be lowest in calories, so you can avoid that dreaded side effect of giving up smoking – weight gain.

This doesn't mean that you can't have steak or lobster; you just have to serve them with large-enough portions of alkaline-forming vegetables to

---

TIP: In tests on smokers, one group of volunteers was given a drug that made their urine more acidic, while another group was given bicarbonate of soda, which made their urine alkaline. The results were dramatic. The acid group virtually chain-smoked throughout the two hours, while the alkaline group chose to smoke no cigarettes at all.

ACID AND ALKALINE-FORMING FOODS

The acids have a negative number and alkalis have a positive number.

Apple, 1 medium	+	4.5
Asparagus, 100g	+	1.2
Avocado, half	+	11.0
Bacon, 1 medium rasher	−	0.4
Banana, 1 medium	+	8.2
Beans, green, 75g	+	5.9
Beef, roast topside, 75g	−	9.4
Bread, white, 1 slice	−	0.9
Bread, wholewheat, 1 slice	−	0.7
Broccoli, 100g	+	10.4
Butter, 1 tablespoon		0
Cheese, Cheddar, 25g	−	1.4
Cheese, Gruyère, 25g	+	1.0
Cheese, Parmesan, 25g	+	1.4
Chicken, roast, 75g	−	11.9
Coffee, 225ml		0
Cornflakes, 25g	−	0.5
Crabmeat, 75g	−	34.0
Cucumber, 50g	+	8.9
Eggs, 1 large	−	9.2
Grapes, 100g	+	8.7
Ham, cold, 75g	−	7.0

Hamburger, lean, 75g	− 9.2
Lamb, roast, 75g	− 8.2
Melon, half cantaloupe	+ 22.4
Milk, whole, 225ml	+ 6.5
Mushrooms, 100g	+ 2.8
Orange juice, 225ml	+ 11.2
Pasta, cooked, 225g	− 2.0
Pear, 1 medium	+ 4.7
Pineapple, 175g	+ 10.9
Potato, boiled, 100g	+ 11.6
Rice, white, cooked, 100g	− 4.8
Salmon, 75g	− 9.4
Shredded Wheat, 1 biscuit	− 1.4
Spinach, 100g	+ 30.5
Tangerine, 1 medium	+ 4.3
Tomato, 1 medium	+ 6.4
Trout, 75g	− 12.9
Walnuts, 25g	− 2.4

make the overall balance of the dish alkaline. For example, if you have a 75g portion of lean roast topside, it has a score of −9.4, but if you serve it with 75g of green beans (+5.9), a medium carrot (+7.3) and a medium tomato (+6.4), then the dish is alkaline.

There's no need to take a calculator out with you and add up the values for every single meal or snack.

Once you understand the basic principles, you can judge for yourself at a glance. As a basic rule of thumb, try to make sure that fruits or vegetables take up two-thirds of the plate and any protein or starches take only one-third or less. Eat a side salad with every main meal and opt for fruit-based desserts. If you want to snack, almonds, brazil nuts, raisins, dates and dried apricots are all good, but peanuts, pecans and walnuts are acid-forming – as are doughnuts and chocolate biscuits!

2. AVOID BLOOD SUGAR SWINGS

Dips in blood sugar can cause fatigue and cravings, while peaks can cause jitteriness and anxiety. The hormone that is causing these swings is insulin, which is produced by the pancreas to help you transport sugars through the blood stream to the sites where it is needed.

Sugars don't just come from chocolate bars and the white granules you stir in your tea. All carbohydrates (bread, rice, pasta, grains, pulses, nuts and vegetables) are broken down in the digestive system to simple sugars (such as glucose and fructose). 'Simple' carbohydrates, such as those in chocolate, are absorbed more quickly than 'complex' ones, such as whole grains, beans, pulses and vegetables.

Refined foods like white bread, cakes and biscuits are high in simple carbohydrates, so if you eat a piece of chocolate cake, a bowl of pasta or a digestive biscuit, the sugars hit your bloodstream in one great rush, triggering the pancreas to produce lots of insulin to mop them up. You feel good with your blood sugar rush – but not for long, because the sugars are mopped up quickly and you feel a dip in energy and a desire to eat more sugar.

Meanwhile, if you eat complex carbohydrates like brown rice or stalky vegetables, the fibre content slows their absorption into the digestive system so it takes longer for the sugars to reach your bloodstream and they are absorbed more slowly and steadily. This way, you can avoid blood sugar highs and lows, and the cravings that go with them.

People who eat a lot of refined carbohydrates and sugars often produce more insulin than they need, meaning the levels in the blood stay high. This encourages the body to store more fat and it has another undesirable side effect as well. As insulin

---

TIP: Base your meals around fruits and vegetables, serving soups, salads and vegetable dishes, with just a little protein or carbo-hydrate on the side.

levels drop after a balanced meal, this triggers the release of serotonin in the brain to let us know that we are full. People with high insulin levels may never experience this cut-off point, so don't feel satisfied by their food.

Stop Smoking Nutrition Plan rule number 1 advised you to cut right back on starches and proteins, so as to maintain an alkaline balance. Rule number 2 is to avoid blood sugar swings by making sure that any starches you do eat are complex, slowly absorbed ones. This means you should eat foods as close to their natural state as possible. An apple with its skin left on will be more slowly absorbed than one without skin, and apple juice will be absorbed more quickly than either. Brown rice, with husks, will be absorbed more slowly than white rice, from which the husks have been removed.

Another tip for maintaining steady blood sugar is to avoid huge, rich meals and try to eat six to eight smaller snacks, one every two to three hours. After more than three hours without eating anything, your blood sugar levels will start to dip, and they'll need a

TIP: In 1997, it was estimated that the British tobacco industry made a profit of £35 million from teenage smokers.

boost again – even if it's just a snack of a handful of sunflower seeds and a few cherries.

3. WHAT'S YOUR POISON?

As you detox from nicotine, tar and all the other toxic chemicals that smoking introduced to your body, it would be a shame to replace them with other harmful substances. Some of the toxins of modern life, such as air pollution, are hard to avoid. We have some say over the ones we put in our mouths, though, so be aware of the poisons in certain everyday foods and drinks.

Keep your diet as simple and fresh as possible, avoiding processed and packaged foods with their bumper helpings of salt, sugar, preservatives, colourings and E additives. Some food additives are implicated in a range of health problems, from asthma to hyperactivity, cancer to immune system malfunctioning. Buy organic as often as you can afford, to avoid pesticide residues on fruits and vegetables and the antibiotics that are routinely fed to farmed animals and fish.

Caffeine, which is present in tea, coffee, chocolate and some fizzy drinks, can exacerbate many of the symptoms of nicotine withdrawal, causing anxiety, insomnia, irritability, depression and panic attacks. If you are suffering from any of these symptoms as you give up smoking, it would be best to minimise your caffeine intake and keep that cup of coffee to mornings only. However, tea – especially green tea – has a high flavonoid content and can decrease the risk of heart disease and stroke, reduce blood pressure and possibly protect against some cancers. Studies have indicated that people who drink four cups of tea a day are 50% less likely to have a heart attack than non-tea drinkers. Those who drink eight to ten cups a day appear to have a lower risk of digestive system, skin and bladder cancers.

You should monitor your alcohol intake closely when you give up smoking, and not just because of its effects on willpower. Both caffeine and alcohol affect you more powerfully after you give up, so you may find you get drunk on less intake. Those who regularly drink more than two or three drinks a day (where one drink = a half pint of beer, a small glass of wine or a single measure of spirits) are often malnourished because they are not absorbing vitamins and

---

TIP: The antioxidants found in green tea can protect against premature ageing of the skin – and your skin may need all the help it can get if you've been smoking for a while.

minerals properly. The same is true of smokers, so if you do both, chances are you already have deficiencies. See rule 4 for how to make them up.

You don't have to become a saint and avoid alcohol altogether when you stop smoking, but keep an eye on your intake. If you like red wine, why not stick to that? It contains some powerful antioxidants (see page 148), can help to reduce stress and possibly lower the risk of heart disease, so long as you stick within the prescribed limits. Alcohol should ideally only be drunk with food to slow its absorption and give your stomach some protection.

HERBAL TEAS

Try some of the vast range of herbal teas on the market, which can have mild medicinal effects as well as being a refreshing, caffeine-free drink. Chamomile is calming, good for relieving headaches and can make you sleepy at bedtime; try peppermint to improve digestion and to help you concentrate; fennel tea is good for detoxing the system; lemon balm helps to relieve depression and anxiety; bilberry tea is good for the eyesight; raspberry leaf tea can help women who suffer from pre-menstrual syndrome; and lemon and ginger can help to ward off viruses and relieve nausea.

4. RE-VITALISE

No matter what technique (or techniques) you have chosen to give up smoking, you can help your body to start repairing itself from Day One by taking a good multivitamin supplement. While you smoke, you are generating excess quantities of 'free radicals' in your bloodstream, which can trigger harmful cell mutations that could result in cancer. Free radicals also cause hardening and furring of the arteries, which causes coronary heart disease; and they are responsible for premature skin ageing, cataracts in the eyes and a number of degenerative diseases.

Antioxidant vitamins A, C and E and the mineral selenium are the body's main defence against free radicals, neutralising them before they cause damage. Riboflavin, copper, manganese and zinc are also good antioxidants. Smokers have loads more free radicals than non-smokers and they don't absorb nutrients so efficiently, so many experts recommend that they take twice the Recommended Daily Allowance (RDA) of antioxidant vitamins. However, smokers shouldn't take high doses of betacarotene, as it seems to increase their lung cancer risk.

To boost your health when you give up smoking, choose a supplement that includes the following:

Vitamin C	150-250mg/day
Vitamin E	50-100mg/day
Carotenoids	15mg/day
Selenium	100mcg/day

Several scientific studies have underlined the benefits of taking daily antioxidant vitamins.

• A ten-year Californian study of 11,000 subjects showed that men taking a high dose of vitamin C daily had a 40% lower risk of getting coronary heart disease and women had a 25% lower risk.

• A study of 87,000 nurses and 40,000 doctors showed that when they took vitamin E supplements for two years, their risk of heart disease was 50% lower for women and 25% lower for men.

• People with high antioxidant intakes have the lowest risk of cancers of the head, neck, stomach, breast, and several other types.

B vitamins are essential for the nervous system's functioning, for energy production and to regulate mood. They are particularly good for relieving nicotine cravings and many of the anxiety-related withdrawal symptoms. You can take the herbal remedy Oatstraw (see page 128) to get a therapeutic dose of B vitamins during the first few weeks of not smoking. Alternatively, make sure your multivitamin contains the following:

Vitamin B1 (thiamine)	1.4mg/day
Vitamin B2 (riboflavin)	1.6mg/day
Vitamin B3 (niacin)	18mg/day
Vitamin B5 (pantothenic acid)	6mg/day
Vitamin B6 (pyridoxine)	2mg/day
Vitamin B12 (cobalamin)	1mcg/day
Folic acid	200mcg/day

Two other substances that you should top up in the immediate aftermath of stopping smoking are lecithin and zinc.

Lecithin (or the choline which is derived from it) helps to break down fats in the bloodstream and boost alertness by stimulating the production of dopamine and noradrenaline in the brain. It eases depression,

---

TIP: Want to find out if you are zinc deficient? Buy a solution of zinc sulphate in the chemist and swish a teaspoon of the liquid round your mouth. If you can't taste it, you probably have zinc deficiency. If it tastes slightly sweet, you have a borderline zinc deficiency, but if it tastes strong and unpleasant, your zinc levels are fine!

improves memory and seems to reduce the risk of coronary heart disease. Take 2-10g of lecithin granules a day, with meals.

Zinc lozenges can stimulate immune cells in the throat and give a boost to the immune responses of the respiratory system. Zinc deficiencies can cause desensitisation of the sense of taste and smell, and can cause gum disease and increase the risk of coronary heart disease. Take 15mg of zinc a day, for a month, to make sure you are not deficient.

IDENTIFY DEFICIENCIES

To get your vitamin and mineral levels analysed and imbalances diagnosed, contact:

Biolab Medical Unit (UK)
Tel: 020 7636 5959
Website: www.biolab.co.uk/tests   or

The Natural Healthcare Centre
Tel: 01283 516444
Website: www.natural-healthcare-centre.co.uk

TIP: Recent studies have found that the amazing anti-cancer properties of broccoli and tomatoes can be increased if you eat the two together.

5. CHOOSE HEALING FOODS

One final tip that can help to heal your body systems, boost your energy and prevent weight gain after you've given up smoking is to avoid 'empty' calories. Make sure every food that passes your lips is contributing vitamins, minerals and health-giving properties, instead of pure sugar, fat and starch. Opt for foods with multiple roles, like the following:

- Apples – they contain vitamin C, an anti-cancer agent called quercetin and pectin, a soluble fibre that lowers blood cholesterol and helps produce regular bowel movements.

- Artichokes – reduce blood cholesterol, improve digestion and protect liver from toxins.

- Asparagus – rich in folate and vitamin E, and contains fructo-oligosaccharide to help the digestive system.

- Avocados – have vitamin E and alphacarotene to prevent furring of the arteries, and omega-6 fats, which are great for the skin.

- Berries – raspberries, strawberries, blackberries and blueberries are all rich in vitamin C, to fight free radicals and prevent heart disease and cancer, and potassium, to aid nerve and muscle function.

- Broccoli – contains glucosinolates, which can fight cancer and help to detoxify the body; also rich in vitamin C, folate and fibre.

- Brown rice – the wholegrain variety contains fibre, magnesium, phosphorus, thiamin and iron.

- Carrots – rich in alphacarotene and betacarotene, which protect against lung cancer; they also help to boost immunity, promote good eyesight and healthy skin, and beat premature ageing.

- Garlic – contains allium, which protects the body from heart disease, high blood pressure, high cholesterol and colon cancer.

- Oats – lots of soluble fibre to improve digestion and lower cholesterol, as well as B vitamins, iron, magnesium and zinc; also good for the regulation of blood sugar and insulin levels.

- Olive oil – lowers harmful cholesterol and protects against cancers, arthritis and heart disease; good source of vitamin E.

- Peppers – contain vitamin C to boost immunity, plus phytochemicals betacrytoxanthin and betacarotene to protect against heart disease.

- Pine nuts – contain protein, monounsaturated oils that are good for the heart, plus vitamin E for the skin.

- Pumpkin seeds – contain omega-3 and omega-6 oils, to protect against heart disease and stroke; omega-3 also reduces joint pain, improves immunity and helps skin.

- Shittake mushrooms – contain lentinan, which boosts defences against cancer, viral and fungal infections; can reduce cholesterol levels and treat many ailments, from diabetes to the common cold.

- Spinach – has iron, betacarotene, folate, vitamin E, vitamin C, plus antioxidant lutein.

- Tomatoes – contain vitamin C, betacarotene and lycopene, a powerful antioxidant that helps to protect against cancer.

- Watercress – chlorophyll boosts circulation; helps to detox the liver and is rich in vitamin C, iron and betacarotene.

AROMATHERAPY

Essential plant oils produced by aromatic plants have many therapeutic properties, ranging from sedative to stimulating, and anti-viral to anti-inflammatory. They are absorbed through the skin or lungs into the bloodstream and tissues, and the scent also works on the limbic system in the brain, which deals directly with emotions, mood and memory. This makes aromatherapy an excellent treatment for stress, anxiety, depression and insomnia, and it's particularly good at promoting a sense of peace and wellbeing when you feel ready to climb the walls.

On another level, aromatherapy can be useful when you give up smoking by reminding you of all the beautiful scents in nature; compare them to the stench of an overflowing ashtray and stale smoke lingering in a room. Aren't you glad you're stopping?

WARNING: If you are pregnant, have high blood pressure, epilepsy or a skin disorder, only use oils prescribed by a qualified aromatherapist. Don't apply oils to broken or damaged skin, and always dilute pure oils before application to the skin. Keep them away from your eyes and don't swallow any, unless in an aromatherapy tea supplied by a therapist.

There are different ways of using aromatherapy oils:

• For a massage, mix 10 drops of essential oil with 2 tablespoons of a carrier oil. (Sweet almond oil, sunflower oil, rapeseed oil and apricot kernel oil are common carriers.)

• Add 5 to 10 drops of pure essential oil to a warm bath.

• Add 2 to 3 drops of pure oil to a bowl of hot water, cover your head with a towel, lean over the bowl and inhale the steam for up to 10 minutes.

• Place 2 or 3 drops on a handkerchief and inhale the scent, or put them on a cotton pad in your pillow.

• Place 2 or 3 drops in an aromatherapy burner, so that the scent evaporates through the room.

• You can also make a warm compress to treat headaches or muscular aches and sprains, by soaking a cloth in a mixture of 5 drops oil to 1 litre of hot water.

Oils all have different properties and they can be used individually or in a blend of up to three oils.

TIP: Women who smoke are at much higher risk of contracting a life-threatening disease than men. It's an unfair world!

Choose ones with the properties you need, but also those whose scent you like. Scent memories vary from individual to individual, and while one person might find that rose oil reminds them of a summer garden in childhood, another may associate it with a funeral, or a place they intensely dislike.

Type of Smoker it Suits

Those who are feeling stressed or anxious after they give up smoking will find aromatherapy calming and relaxing. It can also have useful therapeutic effects, helping to overcome many withdrawal symptoms.

Effectiveness

Aromatherapy definitely has strong stress-relieving qualities. In a clinical test, 100 patients who had just undergone cardiac surgery were divided into four groups. One group was treated with aromatherapy oils, one with dummy oils, one group was counselled by nurses and the fourth group got no support. Those given the aromatherapy treatments were significantly less anxious and more relaxed than the other three groups.

A session with a qualified aromatherapist for a massage with specially chosen essential oils will be the most beneficial experience. Afterwards, you can

AROMATHERAPY OILS TO HELP YOU GIVE UP SMOKING

	Oil	Blends well with	Properties
TOP NOTES	Basil	Bergamot, geranium	A good nerve tonic for anxiety, depression, indecision. Uplifting.
	Bergamot	Cypress, lavender	For anxiety, depression, indigestion, bad breath.
	Clary-sage	Cedarwood, frankincense	Sedative effects for those with anxiety, depression, insomnia.
	Petitgrain	Use alone	Relaxing.
MIDDLE NOTES	Camphor	Frankincense	For depression, insomnia, shock.
	Chamomile	Geranium, lavender	Roman chamomile is sedative, good for irritability, insomnia and nervous tension.
	Cypress	Juniper, sandalwood	Sluggish circulation; coughing; calms irritability.
	Geranium	Almost all oils	Anti-depressant, good for stress-related disorders.
	Juniper	Cypress,	Useful for an anxious state of mind. Stimulates

		...cature and ... urinary, sleep, exertion, insomnia and ailments that are due to nervous problems.
Marjoram	Bergamot, lavender	Lowers high blood pressure, helps constipation, relieves catarrh, calms anxiety and irritability.
Rosemary	Basil, cedarwood	Relieves constipation and mental fatigue, helps to strengthen memory, good for muscular aches and pains.
Thyme	Bergamot, rosemary	A good nerve tonic, can protect against colds and flu, stimulates circulation.
Cedarwood	Cypress, juniper	Good for chronic anxiety; relieves catarrh and coughs.
Frankincense	Camphor, geranium	Eases anxiety , relieves catarrh, rejuvenates.
Rose	Clary-sage, sandalwood	Stimulates circulation, good for constipation and digestive problems caused by stress, helps depression and insomnia.
Sandalwood	Cypress, frankincense	Good for stress-related conditions, such as depression and insomnia.
Ylang-ylang	Most oils	For high blood pressure, depression, insomnia, stress.

BASE NOTES

ask the therapist's advice on oils to use yourself, at home. Alternatively, make your own selection from the list on pages 158-9, perhaps choosing one top note, one middle note and one base note. Top notes are the fastest-acting and base notes last the longest.

Compatibility

Combine aromatherapy with any other quit-smoking techniques, but if you are receiving homeopathic treatment, check with your homeopath first.

CONTACT

To find an aromatherapist, contact:

Aromatherapy Consortium
Tel: 0870 7743477
Website: www.aromatherapy-regulation.org.uk

Most good chemists and health-food shops stock a range of aromatherapy oils, but if you have trouble finding the ones you want, contact:

Neal's Yard Remedies
Tel: 0845 2623145
Website: www.nealsyardremedies.com   or

Tisserand
Tel: 01273 325666
Website: www.tisserand.com

FLOWER REMEDIES

Dr Edward Bach, a Harley Street doctor and homeopath in the 1930s, noticed that patients with the same patterns of negative emotions seemed to suffer the same kinds of ailments. He developed his 38 basic flower remedies to deal with specific mental states, arguing that if you heal the mind first, the body will follow. Since his death, many other healers have developed further types of flower remedies, and Australian Bush Flower Essences, based on ancient Aboriginal medicines, have become increasingly popular in the West.

Many complementary practitioners (especially herbalists and homeopaths) will recommend flower essences, or you can consult a therapist who specialises in them. Alternatively, you can self-prescribe but you need to analyse your mental state carefully and choose the predominant characteristic at the time. If you are not sure, you can use more than one remedy – they are completely harmless – but it is recommended that no more than five are taken at any one time.

Flower remedies are taken by dropping two or three drops onto your tongue, four to six times a day. Alternatively, you can dissolve the drops in water and drink it. The healing essence of the flowers is dissolved in alcohol, so if you are avoiding alcohol you can apply the drops to the pulse points on your wrist instead.

The best-known flower remedy is the ever-popular Dr Bach's Rescue Remedy, a blend of Cherry Plum (for feelings of desperation), Rock Rose (to ease fear and panic), Impatiens (to soothe irritability and tension), Clematis (to counteract the tendency to drift away from the present) and Star of Bethlehem (for the mental and physical symptoms of shock). Rescue Remedy works quickly and effectively in emergency situations involving acute emotional shock, grief and stress. It's a good medicine cabinet standby at any time, and might be worth keeping in your pocket or desk drawer for the first few days after you give up smoking, for moments when you feel on the verge of cracking up.

Type of Smoker it Suits
Flower remedies are particularly effective for those who smoke for emotional reasons or to help them deal with everyday stress. They are faster-acting and easier to use than aromatherapy oils when you're away from home, making them the perfect any-time, any-place antidote to cravings and feelings of anxiety.

FLOWER REMEDIES TO HELP YOU STOP SMOKING
BUSH FLOWER ESSENCES:

Boronia – for obsessive thoughts, so it's great for addictions and addictive behaviour. It helps with concentration and clears the way for new patterns.

Bottlebrush – promotes serenity and calm, and encourages the capacity to cope. It helps to brush away the past and encourages you to embrace new situations.

Mountain devil – great for irritability and anger. It is also good for detoxification and deep cleansing of the system.

BACH FLOWER REMEDIES:

Clematis – to help day-dreamers and the absent-minded improve their concentration and pull their thoughts back to the present.

Crab apple – a cleansing remedy for those who feel unclean or polluted, either physically or emotionally, and who need a purification ritual.

Impatiens – for impatience and irritability. Good for those who are always in a hurry and too busy to slow down.

Mustard – for depression, especially depression that descends for no particular reason.

Scleranthus – for those who are indecisive, lack concentration and suffer from mood swings.

Effectiveness

One study reported by the Flower Essence Society involved a group of subjects exposed to the stress of strong fluorescent lights. The group taking flower essences showed far less brain activity and muscle tension than those who weren't taking anything, showing that flower essences made the experience much less stressful.

Compatibility

You can use flower essences with any other quit-smoking therapy, but if you are receiving homeopathic treatments, you should tell your homeopath.

CONTACT

To find a Dr Bach-trained practitioner, contact

Dr Edward Bach Centre
Tel: 01491 834678
Website: www.bachcentre.com

To buy flower essences by mail order:

Flower Essence Repertoire
Tel: 01428 741672

Nelson's Pharmacy
Tel: 0207 495 2404

BEHAVIOUR MODIFICATION

If you are the kind of smoker who often finds a cigarette in your hand without any awareness of having lit it, or if you automatically reach for a pack in certain situations, you might benefit from a therapy that teaches you to re-train your behaviour.

There are several kinds of counselling and psychotherapy that work in different ways. Some of them delve into childhood experiences to try and explain your current state of mind; but if you simply want to quit smoking without any other kind of analysis, you should opt for one of the behaviour-based therapies. These include:

- Behavioural therapy, which works on the principle that behaviour is learned in response to past experience and can be unlearned or reconditioned without analysing the past to uncover that reason.

- Cognitive therapy uses the power of the mind to influence behaviour. You are taught to recognise and change negative or self-destructive behaviours, and reverse habitual behaviour patterns.

- Cognitive behavioural therapy uses a mixture of behavioural and cognitive therapy to help change ingrained ways of thinking and behaving. The treatment may involve learning some relaxation techniques.

• Neurolinguistic programming works on the theory that our life experiences from birth onwards have programmed the way in which we see the world. An NLP therapist will help you to look at ways you have learned to think and feel, so that you are better able to take control of your own actions. You may be taught to change your body language, and to alter the way you speak, to help enhance your communication skills and bring about change in various aspects of your life.

• Brief (solution-based) therapy focuses solely on the problem that you bring along, and teaches you techniques to deal with it. It would normally consist of just three or four sessions, possibly with a follow-up in three months' time.

TIP: When choosing a therapist, have a brief chat on the phone with them first and assess whether you find them easy to talk to and sympathetic. There aren't hard and fast demarcation lines between most of the different behavioural approaches, and a good therapist will assess you individually and choose a technique that suits your needs.

What Happens at a Consultation?

Each therapist will have their own approaches, but a first step will be to talk about why you smoke, how you smoke, when you smoke and the mental associations you have with smoking. Substances become psychologically addictive if they provide a kind of support that you need, or help you to express something that would otherwise stay hidden. The problem is that nicotine addiction makes you ill while fulfilling this need, so you have to develop more effective, harmless ways of meeting your deep, underlying needs on a daily basis.

For example, if you have a frantically busy life, it may be that stopping for a cigarette is the one time when you allow yourself to relax and be still. The therapist will help you to separate 'smoking' from 'relaxation' and find another way to give yourself time out, in which you achieve the same state of calm. This is not as simple as direct substitution, because you need to access your subconscious for the relaxation to be truly effective.

Some therapists might suggest finding a physical trigger – a posture or movement – that creates a sense memory. Think about the posture you sit in when you are in a relaxed state, the way you stare unfocused into the distance or out of the window, and how you arrange your arms. Find a movement that is your anchor, your way of accessing this state of relaxation. Perhaps it might simply be learning how to relax a tight jaw. Once you have fixed this in your brain, in future you will be able to get into the relaxed state automatically simply by relaxing your jaw and staring into the distance. This technique will soon teach you a deeper kind of relaxation than you ever achieved with smoking.

Similarly, if smoking used to help you feel at ease at a party or social event, you will find some kind of postural trick to access the more confident state you used to reach through smoking. If you smoke when you are emotionally upset, you'll learn a new behavioural technique for comforting and nurturing yourself. Perhaps you enjoy the ritual of smoking, with all the paraphernalia of ashtray and lighter, and the feeling of belonging to a 'club' with other smokers.

TIP: Try the following technique whenever you feel anxious. With one palm facing upwards, use the fingers of the other hand to press a point on the little-finger side of your arm, about an inch below the wrist bone towards the elbow. Massage in tiny circles for a minute or so. It might ache at first but, as the sensation shifts, so will your anxiety. This technique can help relieve panic attacks.

In this case, a behavioural technique could help you to develop a new and healthier ritual.

It's a mistake to take away the habit without dealing with the causes, because more likely than not, a new habit will take its place. This is what happens when ex-smokers start to over-eat, or drink more alcohol, or manically chew gum after they give up. They may have got over their physical addiction to nicotine, but the mental addiction to smoking remains.

In a cognitive therapy session, you'll be taught to hold up negative statements and beliefs and examine them in the light of day. For example, if you tend to think that you won't be able to quit smoking because you're too dependent on it, you might be taught to examine this belief and reframe it in a positive way: 'I used to think I wouldn't be able to quit but millions of people have managed it, so I can too.' If you secretly believe that smoking calms you down and you'll be a nervous wreck without it, you'll learn to say: 'I used to think that smoking made me calmer but now that I understand how nicotine works, I realise that I will be much more calm once I am a non-smoker.'

TIP: People under the age of 40 are five times more likely to have a heart attack if they smoke than if they are non-smokers.

QUIT MASTERS

After a one-hour session with a Quit Masters trainer, 95% of clients are smoke-free and the other 5% are invited to return until they beat their habit as well. They use a combination of hypnotherapy and neuro-linguistic programming to work on the subconscious and conscious minds together. You are taught to substitute your unhealthy habit, in this case smoking, for a healthy alternative, like exercise, or drinking a glass of water, or deep breathing. They say that the key to their success lies in their identification of each individual's motives for giving up, and an analysis of their belief system about smoking, then the session is tailored to suit each specific case. You are also given techniques to use afterwards and, under hypnosis, you are given a colour. Every time you see that colour in the future, it will reaffirm to you that you are a non-smoker.

To find your nearest Quit Masters centre and get more information about the course, contact:

Tel: 0800 2985155

SELF-DESTRUCTIVE BEHAVIOUR

If you have other addictions as well as smoking, and habitually behave in ways that you know are dangerous or bad for you, you may need counselling or psychotherapy to help you unravel your motives. Sometimes self-destructive behaviour is an attempt to mask emotional pain by creating real physical pain, and in this case a therapist would gently help you to pinpoint the cause of the emotional pain and work to heal that, rather than addressing your destructive habits straight away.

Some people who self-harm are punishing themselves because they don't feel they deserve any better. Their self-esteem is at rock bottom; they believe they're not successful or clever or witty or attractive, so they might as well not be healthy either. There can be all kinds of causes for this lack of self-belief, but it is likely that they had an insecure relationship with their main carer during childhood, which a therapist can help them to understand.

Some people seem to be afraid of success, and they sabotage themselves just before the last hurdle. It gives them an excuse to fail. But why not think it through and learn how to succeed instead?

People who are prone to addictions quite often report a feeling of emptiness inside. There's something missing, life feels as though it has no meaning, and they smoke, or drink, or take drugs to mask this disturbing sensation. A good therapist can help you to confront the emptiness and find your own ways of giving life meaning, which could be through creativity or spirituality, or perhaps by giving something back to the world. For more on this, see page 252.

If any of these patterns sound like you, therapy could be enormously helpful and could turn your whole life around very quickly. Deal with your self-image problems first, and it will be a whole lot easier to tackle your smoking habit later, when you no longer need it as a shield.

Type of Smoker it Suits

If you are a habitual smoker and have failed to quit in the past because you never got through the mental addiction, then behavioural modification could provide the breakthrough you need. If you are self-destructive in other ways apart from smoking, consider talking to a counsellor or psychotherapist.

Effectiveness

Behaviour modification techniques can help you to dump a decades-old smoking habit without looking backwards. With all kinds of therapy, if you get a good counsellor that you feel in tune with, results can be dramatic and the improvements to your quality of life can be massive.

Compatibility

If you are seeing a hypnotherapist, discuss it with your behaviour modification therapist as their treatments may overlap. Otherwise, it can work alongside any other therapy in this book.

CONTACT

To find a therapist, contact

The British Association of Counselling and Psychotherapy
Tel: 0870 443 5252
Website: bacp.co.uk

TIP: Smoking increases the risk of impotence for men in their 30s and 40s by around 50%. The British Medical Association estimates that 12,000 British men in this age group are impotent because they smoke.

SUPPORT GROUPS

There are NHS stop-smoking support groups all over the country, and free help could be just one phone call away. Some areas run courses or programmes and certain clinics provide one-to-one support, while others just offer the opportunity to share your experiences with a group of other people who are going through the same thing.

You may feel shy about sharing your thoughts and fears with a roomful of strangers but once you get there, you will find the other group members welcoming you and striving to put you at your ease. The best advice is to find out about all the groups within easy reach of your home and try several, because each may have a different approach or a different type of membership. Don't give up if you try one and don't feel comfortable; the tone of meetings tends to be set by the group leader, and the next one you try could have a completely different feel.

Some people at a group will already have given up smoking, while others are just building up to another

---

TIP: If you feel nervous about attending a support group, you should realise that most of the people there will be at least as nervous as you.

attempt. Wherever you are, you should pick up advice and tools that help you, and the group ethos will reinforce your resolve. It can work in the same ways that WeightWatchers works for dieters; partly they persevere because they don't want to be seen to fail in front of the rest of the group.

Hardened, dyed-in-the-wool smokers might like to try a Nicotine Anonymous group, based on the very successful 12-step model used by Alcoholics Anonymous. There you are encouraged to admit that your addiction is out of control and surrender your will to a higher power (which can derive from whatever belief system you may hold). You listen to people who have succeeded and those who are still struggling, and you can share your experiences or ask advice from the others, as you wish. Part of the 'cure' involves helping others, so you will be encouraged to stay involved once you have given up smoking yourself. So far Nicotine Anonymous groups are only found in the London area, but this may change – or you could talk to them about starting a group in your home town.

The charity Quit have a telephone and e-mail helpline, which you can use as frequently as you need to, and they will organise corporate support groups to visit your company or groups of professionals, on request. Courses can be tailor-made, with advice that is specifically suited to your profession.

Type of Smoker they Suit

If you are struggling to quit on your own, a group could provide the impetus you lack. Everyone there will be willing you to succeed, and will provide emotional support as well as behavioural advice, depending on what you need. At NHS clinics, they will also be able to prescribe nicotine replacements or Zyban, if they think it would be helpful in your case.

Effectiveness

So long as you keep attending and don't walk out after a couple of smoke-free days, you should find the moral support provided by a group invaluable. It could work on many levels, but once you know some people at your local group, you may just stay off tobacco out of a sense of pride and not wanting them to see you fail. The reason doesn't matter, so long as you can sustain it.

Compatibility

You can attend a support group while trying any of the other techniques described in this book, although the advice you are given there may not be the same as that given by an Allen Carr clinic, or a homeopath, for example. It's a good idea to combine physical therapies, such as herbalism or nicotine replacement, with a mental one like group support.

CONTACT

ASH (for free NHS clinics)
Helpline: 0800 169 0169 (they also have helplines in Asian languages)
Website: www.ash.org.uk

ASH Northern Ireland
Helpline: 02890 663281

ASH Scotland
Tel: 0800 848484

ASH Wales
Tel: 0345 697 500

QUIT (an independent charity)
Tel: 0800 002200
E-mail: info@quit.org.uk
Website: www.quit.org.uk

Nicotine Anonymous
Tel: 020 7976 0076
Website: www.nicotine-anonymous.org

BREATHING

Smokers tend to take short breaths from the top of their lungs and don't expel them completely when they breathe out. This may be because their lungs have lost some elasticity from years of being coated in tar, or it may be because deep breaths can cause spasms of coughing, as the movement of the lungs loosens phlegm. The problem is that shallow breaths don't deliver oxygen into the bloodstream so efficiently and they don't get rid of carbon monoxide build-up either. The deepest breath many smokers ever take is when they light a new cigarette and inhale that first drag deeply to get the most effective nicotine buzz they can.

Learning to breathe properly, with full inhalations and exhalations, has dozens of benefits for all the muscles in your body, including the heart, and it is one of the best methods of stress relief. If you learn deep breathing while you are giving up smoking, it will help to clear your lungs of toxins, give you masses of extra energy, improve your brain function and circulation, and help you to cope with nicotine cravings as well. Once you can visualise and feel the muscles working in your

TIP: Remember the golden rule: nothing can be so bad that a cigarette won't make it worse.

chest, controlling the movements of your lungs, you are less likely to want to clog them up with tar again.

CELEBRITY SMOKERS

It's usually easy to tell smokers from non-smokers when you see them talking (or singing) on television. The smokers have husky, deep voices that seem to come from the throat rather than from the diaphragm. Watch out for pop stars with tendons standing out on their necks while they strain to reach the notes and project their voices. Compare them with professional opera singers and classically trained theatre actors, effortlessly filling an auditorium with the sound of their voices. Those with trained voices have strengthened their breathing muscles and learned to use them effectively – and it's very rare for them to be smokers.

Stand in front of a mirror and watch yourself breathing. Do your shoulders or collarbone move upwards or the muscles in your neck tense as you breathe in? This is a sure sign that you're breathing from the top of your lungs only. The way it should work is that when you breathe in, your ribs expand outwards and backwards and the muscles in your abdomen lengthen. When you breathe out, the abdominal muscles shorten, pulling the ribs downwards. Your shoulders and neck should not be involved.

Different therapies and exercise regimes teach different ways of breathing, but all of them work to strengthen the muscles that control breathing, helping the lungs to expand and contract fully each time. There are five simple breathing exercises described in this section. Try them when you are giving up smoking, and see how quickly you get better at them.

Expanding the Ribs

1. Sit straight in a chair with your head up and shoulders relaxed, then place the heels of your hands on your lower ribs, just below your armpits. As you breathe in, feel your hands being pushed outwards. As you breathe out, feel them move in and down.

2. Still keeping your hands on your ribs, breathe in through your nose to a count of 4 and breathe out through your mouth to a count of 4. Next breathe in and out to a count of 6, then try 8 and finally 10, if you can manage it. Keep it steady and rhythmic and stop if you feel dizzy.

Breathing into your Back

The intercostal muscles running between the ribs in your sides and back are often underused, but some deep breathing can give them a good stretch and ease muscle tension throughout your upper back.

1. Sit on a stool with your back straight, shoulders relaxed and arms by your sides. As you breathe in, imagine you are inflating a beachball between your shoulderblades and try to direct your breath into it. Don't let your shoulders curve forward. It takes some practice to get the hang of this but it's a great feeling when you breathe deeply enough to stretch the muscles in your back.

2. Count slowly to 4 as you breathe into your back, and 4 as you breathe out.

Abdominal Breathing

1. Lie on your back with your knees bent, feet on the floor, and your head supported by a small cushion or a folded towel. Place one hand on your abdomen and one on your upper chest.

2. Breathe in deeply through your nose, letting your breath go into the abdomen first, then your lower ribs and finally your chest. This means that the hand on your chest should remain still while the hand on your abdomen is pushed upwards. Feel all the muscles between your ribs opening out.

TIP: There are about 12 million cigarette smokers in the UK and 1.3 million who smoke pipes or cigars.

3. When you exhale, draw in the abdomen first, then the ribs and finally the upper chest. Practise until you can establish a flowing wave-like pattern of expansion and contraction, breathing in to a count of 8 and out to a count of 8.

Breathing for Energy

1. Sit on the floor with your legs loosely crossed, the backs of your hand resting on your knees and your head bent forwards. Breathe in, stretching your spine, drawing up your abdomen and opening and lifting the chest, filling it with air up to the collarbones. Don't raise your shoulders.

2. As you breathe out, keep your chest lifted and your spine stretched, letting the breath trickle out gradually, as if by itself. Repeat six times, but stop at any time if you feel dizzy.

Cleansing Breath

1. Sit cross-legged on the floor, as before. Breathe in then sharply contract your abdominal muscles to force air out of your lungs through your nose.

2. Relax your abdominal muscles and let air flow back into your lungs, keeping your mouth closed. Repeat this six times.

LEARNING TO BREATHE

It's a great idea to take up some kind of activity that requires you to learn a specific form of breathing when you give up smoking. Picturing the action of the lungs and becoming aware of the way the muscles work when you breathe means you will be less likely to want to reintroduce noxious substances to your respiratory system. Here are some suggestions you might want to try:

- All kinds of yoga use specific breathing techniques to enhance the movements. For example, astanga yoga uses a method called ujjayi breathing, a calm cleansing breath which is achieved by partially closing the back of the throat and sucking air in and out, making a noise like waves on a seashore.

TO FIND A YOGA TEACHER, CONTACT

Website: www.yoga.co.uk   or

Astanga Yoga London
Tel: 07747 824178
Website: www.astangayoga.co.uk

The British Wheel of Yoga
Tel: 01529 306851
Website: www.bwy.org.uk

- Pilates is a gentle but very effective exercise technique that uses breathing to assist the movements. You breathe in through your nose and out through your mouth, controlling the exhalation to suit the length of the movement. Dancers and performers use Pilates to stay in shape while preventing injury.

TO FIND A PILATES TEACHER, CONTACT

The Pilates Foundation
Tel: 07071 781559
Website: www.pilatesfoundation.com

Alan Herdman Studios
Tel: 020 7723 9953
Website: www.alanherdmanpilates.co.uk

- Alexander Technique re-educates your posture and teaches you how to use your body more efficiently. As you learn how to align your head, neck and spine, your breathing naturally becomes easier and your voice becomes more powerful. The technique is favoured by actors in particular.

TO FIND AN ALEXANDER TEACHER, CONTACT

The Society of Teachers of Alexander Technique
Tel: 020 7283 3338
Website: www.stat.org.uk

- Buteyko is a breathing technique that was developed especially for those with illnesses caused or exacerbated by poor breathing, such as asthma, sinusitis, snoring, panic attacks and emphysema. At Buteyko lessons you will be taught how to perform a series of breathing exercises that can relieve many symptoms of illness.

> **TO FIND A BUTEYKO TEACHER, CONTACT**
> **The Buteyko Breathing Association**
> Tel: 01277 364724
> www.buteykobreathing.org

- When you train your voice, either as an actor, singer or public speaker, you learn to breathe from your diaphragm and use the bottom and sides of your lungs. If you are interested in taking voice lessons, contact your nearest music or drama college and they will be able to recommend a teacher if they don't run courses themselves.

TIP: Some therapists believe that negative emotions we haven't dealt with can tighten the diaphragm, and regular deep breathing can help to shift them.

MEDITATIONS AND VISUALISATIONS

Meditation used to be associated in most people's minds with Buddhism, or yoga, or the Maharishi Mahesh Yogi who introduced The Beatles to Transcendental Meditation (TM). In fact, it can be a simple, stand-alone skill, without any greater universal significance, that you can use at any time to calm yourself down and feel centred. It's quite tricky to learn, and the more you practise the better you'll get, but there are some very simple techniques that anyone can benefit from even if they've never meditated before.

Meditation has loads of benefits for your health and can assist you in your stop-smoking plan by giving you a way to deal with stress, treat depression and feel focused. The pattern of brainwaves changes while you are meditating, from busy beta-waves to slower alpha-waves, and there are a number of physical benefits that come with regular practice: blood pressure and cholesterol levels are lowered, arteries blocked with plaque can begin to clear, and adrenaline levels drop, meaning there is less pressure on the cardiovascular system.

You don't need special tools to meditate. It can be done in your office during lunch hour, in your bedroom first thing in the morning, in a field, on the bus or even in the dentist's chair. Some systems teach you to focus on a candle or other object; in transcendental meditation you are given your own mantra to chant; but one of the simplest methods to learn is to focus on your breathing, feeling all the sensations of air flowing in through your nostrils, and your chest expanding then contracting again as the air flows out. To relax into the meditative state, it can help to count your breath in and out.

Some systems will insist that you sit cross-legged on the floor, straight-backed, without leaning against anything. If you do this, note that it helps to sit on a small cushion, which will tilt your pelvis forward, letting your hips open more easily and your knees come closer to the ground. If you prefer, you can meditate lying down on cushions or sitting in a comfortable chair. The main thing is to make sure that you will be undisturbed for 20 minutes or so, that the room is quiet and warm, and that your clothing is loose enough to allow you to breathe freely.

When you first start, just let yourself sit still, with your eyes shut, following the rise and fall of your own breathing. Count each inhalation and exhalation, making them regular and flowing. At first you will find your mind wandering to errands you haven't done, or an argument you had the day before, or what you're planning to have for dinner. Think of your meditation as a river flowing steadily along within its banks; when an external distraction comes into your head, imagine it is like a tree branch floating on the surface of the water and you must pick it out and place it on the bank so that the river can continue smoothly on its course. More distractions will come, but gently lift each one out and continue on your way.

Meditation is an extremely useful skill for anyone to learn and it can be particularly useful for dealing with stress and anxiety after you give up smoking. There are some sample meditations below, but you will find it more effective to learn from a teacher in the first instance.

CONTACT

To find a meditation teacher, contact:

The Vipassana Trust
Tel: 01989 730234
www.dhamma.org   or

The Transcendental Meditation Association
Tel: 0870 5143733

A QUICK MIDDAY MEDITATION

Sit cross-legged on the floor, supporting your hips with a small cushion. Rest your hands on your knees, palms down, and relax your shoulders. Make sure your spine is straight but not rigid. Pull back your chin slightly. Close your eyes and open your mouth a little, letting your jaw relax downwards. Touch the tip of your tongue to the gums just behind your top front teeth, and run it along the ridges.

Breathe in gently through your nose, feeling the air in your nostrils. Breathe out again through your nose. Focus on your breath until it becomes more and more peaceful, soft and gentle, almost as though it is flowing by itself without any help from you.

Think about the sensations in your body and, if you sense any tensions anywhere, direct your breath to smooth them out. Are you holding tension between your eyebrows? Breathe in and let the breath smooth your brows. Is there tension in your temples? Is it

TIP: If you would like to learn more by yourself, a book called *Teach Yourself to Meditate*, by Eric Harrison, is a valuable guide for beginners. So is *Meditation for Dummies* by Stephan Bodian (despite the offputting name!). You can also buy some lovely meditation tapes and, if you're keen, you can go on meditation retreats.

more on one side than the other? Feel the breath ease it away. Move down to your lips then your jaws, rubbing out any tightness with your warm peaceful breaths.

Continue down into your neck and shoulders, breathing into the knots, smoothing out tension in the muscles, making them completely relaxed. You may become aware of a sensation in your knee, or hip, or foot; simply observe it, breathe in and direct your breath to relieve the tightness. Keep your breathing slow and rhythmic.

When you have smoothed all the tensions in your muscles, sit for a while longer before you gradually bring yourself back to the tasks of the day.

THE INSOMNIA MEDITATION

This slow, methodical meditation uses breath counting as you scan each part of the body in turn. If your thoughts wander off, bring them back again to the part you have reached. It's rare for anyone to get through all three parts of this meditation without falling asleep.

Lie on your back in bed with your arms by your sides and your head supported by a small pillow. Close your eyes. Breathe in and think about the little finger of your right hand. How does it feel? Don't move it, but be aware that it is possible to increase the flow of blood to a part of the body just by thinking about it. Breathe out.

Breathe in and think about the fourth finger of your right hand. Breathe out. Breathe in and focus on the third finger. Breathe out. Continue the same breathing pattern as you think about your second finger, thumb, the back of your hand, the palm of your hand, your wrist, your right forearm, your elbow, your upper arm, your shoulder, your neck, the right side of your upper ribs, the right side of your lower ribs, your abdomen, right hip, right thigh, knee, lower leg, right ankle, heel, sole of foot, top of foot, little toe, fourth toe, third toe, second toe, big toe.

Breathe deeply and be aware how much heavier the right side of your body feels after you have scanned it. Let it sink deeper into the mattress. Feel the way all the muscles have relaxed totally, while the left side is still lighter, more alert.

TIP: Smokers' wounds don't heal as well as non-smokers'. A study followed 120 women, including 69 smokers, who had a minor operation. Months later, the smokers' scars were three times as wide as the non-smokers'.

Breathe in and out a few times then, when you're ready, do the same scan down the left side of your body, starting with the little finger of your left hand and moving down to the big toe on the left foot. Gradually you will feel the left side getting heavier and sinking deeper into the mattress to match the right side. If your thoughts wander off, bring them back again to the breathing and thinking about which part of the body you have reached.

When you finish scanning the left side, your body will feel very relaxed, very heavy. Breathe in and out a few times, experiencing the sensation of sinking down, deeper and deeper into the bed.

When you are ready, breathe in and think about the crown of your head, the very top point of your skull. Breathe out. Breathe in and think about your temples. Breathe out. Continue with the breathing pattern as you focus on your forehead, eyebrows, eyelids, cheekbones, nose, ears, upper lip, jaw, and then move inside your body, going with the breath.

Breathe in and think about your tongue. Breathe out. Focus on your throat, your lungs, your heart, your stomach, the coils of your digestive system, your liver, your kidneys, until you can feel all your internal organs are relaxed as well. Keep breathing and feeling the heaviness, and sinking deeper and deeper down into the bed.

PLACEBOS

Placebos are pills with no active ingredients, but they can have a strong healing effect because they harness the power of the mind. Between 30 and 70% of sick people taking placebos report an abatement of their symptoms, and sometimes show quite dramatic results. These people are not gullible; quite the reverse, as the placebo response seems to be strongest in well-educated, self-reliant types. What they are doing is imagining that the pills will work, then the power of their thoughts seems to positively influence the outcome.

CLEANSING VISUALISATION

This one is especially designed for when you give up smoking, and it's a journey for your mind to help cleanse the body after all those years of inhaling tar and toxic chemicals. Read it through first then start with a simple relaxation exercise, like the Quick Midday Meditation, to get you into a deeply relaxed state. You don't need to cross your legs – just sit somewhere comfortable, close your eyes and let yourself slow down and focus on your thoughts.

Imagine that you are putting on a pair of special X-ray specs that will allow you to look inside your body and see what all the years of smoking have done to it. Keep breathing steadily in and out as you think about all the damage you might see. Now you are going to travel into your own body, flowing inside with your breath and down into your lungs. The pink sponginess has been obscured by tough black soot, like an old clogged-up fireplace, but you have a magic cloth with which you can rub and polish all the inside surfaces, all the branches and grooves, inlets and folds. As you rub away the filthy blackness, it evaporates and is exhaled from your body, dissolving into nothing in the air outside. Rub and polish the first lung until it is pink and spongy again, without a trace of black, then move over to the other lung, rubbing gently but persistently until every last patch of black has vanished and your lungs are fresh and springy again. Your breathing feels easier now, without any tightness.

Just as oxygen crosses from the lungs into the bloodstream, you will now do the same, taking your magic cloth with you. As you approach the heart, you notice that the arteries are clogged up with deposits of plaque. Some of it has hardened, like the limescale that clogs pipes in hard water areas; some of it is sticky, like lard. Use your magic cloth to wipe the plaque free from the artery walls and let it dissolve in the blood, ready to be cleansed completely from the body by your liver and kidneys. As you clear the plaque from each of the main arteries, the heart has to work less hard to pump blood; its movements become slower and easier, more fluid and rhythmic.

After you have cleansed the main blood vessels round the heart, relax and let your bloodstream carry you on a journey round your body. Where you find that blood vessels have constricted, push your magic cloth into the narrow tubes to open them up and let the blood flow again. Wipe away any more plaque deposits that you find. Notice that the blood is a deeper, richer shade of red now that oxygen is being carried efficiently by the red blood cells. Go right down into your ankles and feet, round the toes and then back up your calves, opening up all the constricted arteries and veins along the way.

Now let the blood take you into your liver and polish away any toxins that have built up, rubbing them until they dissolve. If the liver has been under a heavy strain, parts of it may look tired and rotten, but give them a polish and watch as they clear themselves out and spring back to health. Now go to your kidneys and polish them clean until they sparkle; from now on they will be able to release all the toxins from your body, without becoming stained themselves.

Finally, let the blood flow back up through your body and into your head. Use the magic cloth to rub clean all the grooves and crinkles in your brain, letting it know that it will no longer have to wait for the stimulus of nicotine to do its work. The nicotine has gone and your organs are healthy and shining, ready to function by themselves, doing all the complex, carefully balanced tasks allocated to each, powered by clean, oxygenated blood flowing smoothly round your body, taking nutrients to the places that need them, from the brain, to the skin, to the digestive system, to the toes.

Breathe out and let the breath bring you back out of your head, to the place where you are sitting. Breathe slowly for a few moments then gradually bring yourself round.

VISUALISATION FOR SUCCESS

Positive visualisations are a powerful tool, often used in sports psychology and business motivational courses. When Tiger Woods has to make one putt to win the championship, he stops and visualises hitting the ball with exactly the right pressure and watching it roll across the green and drop into the hole; then he does it. Top businessmen are taught to visualise the deal being agreed, contracts signed, hands being shaken, before they go forward with confidence and close that deal.

Research studies over the last decades have consistently shown visualisation to be effective in every area of life, from health to work to social life to love. The trick is simple: before any event or activity, visualise yourself performing exactly as you want to. When you get sick, visualise yourself being well again. There have been some remarkable stories of cancer patients visualising a battle between invading cancer cells and their own more powerful immune cells, which the immune cells win; studies report that patients using this technique live an average of a year longer than those who don't.

Try a positive visualisation concerning your stopping smoking. Use the images or symbols that work best for you. If you like, you could envisage a battle against some giant cigarettes, as the nicotine gum television ads did. A more effective example might go as follows.

Think about the past, when you were smoking, as an industrial wasteland where stunted trees, grey skies and withered grass are all covered with a thick layer of ash. The smell is of stale smoke and old ashtrays. You feel lethargic and unhealthy and don't have the energy to do much except sit around feeling gloomy.

Now imagine a wall, a fairly high one. Somehow, after a lot of effort, you have managed to climb it and you are sitting on the top. On the other side of the wall you can see green fields, running water, sunshine, beautifully scented flowers and tall healthy trees reaching up into bright blue sky. Look carefully and you will see a figure walking along a path, moving away from you through the fresh sunny landscape. The person has a spring in their step and is moving forward happily, with a sense of purpose. That person is you in the future. That is who you are going to be. Now look back one last time at the industrial landscape of the past. You will never have to go back there again. Jump down from the wall into the green, sunny side and start to walk into your own positive future.

TIP: Think ahead to situations in which you always used to smoke and visualise yourself being a proud non-smoker. Imagine saying 'No, thank you' when someone hands round a pack in the pub; enjoying the flavours of your food at a meal out instead of lighting up between courses; and being more effective at work because you don't have to zip out for a fag every hour or so.

RELAXATION THERAPIES

If you have been the kind of smoker who slumped in an armchair with a cigarette and a glass of something wet to help you relax at the end of a long day, you will benefit from exploring some healthier methods of relaxation after you give up. Meditation is an invaluable stress-relieving tool, hypnotherapy can teach you how to deal with your own high stress levels and exercise can be very effective for washing away the cares of the day. Some other therapies that might be worth looking into are described below.

MASSAGE

Why not treat yourself to a weekly massage, to shift toxins from the tissues and relieve muscle tension? Some massage therapists believe that repressed emotions are held in the muscles and can be released through the kneading and stroking movements. Try a few different types of massage – such as Swedish, Shiatsu, Thai, Tui-na, Aromatherapy, or Indian head massage – and see which you enjoy the most.

TO FIND A QUALIFIED THERAPIST, CONTACT
The British Complementary Medicine Association
Tel: 0845 3455977
www.bcma.co.uk/massage_therapy

REFLEXOLOGY

Reflexologists believe that by applying pressure to reflex points in the feet and hands, they can stimulate the body's healing mechanisms to relieve tension and cure ailments. The techniques are especially effective for those suffering from stress, fatigue, digestive problems or general muscular or joint aches and pains.

The therapist will ask questions about your medical history and lifestyle before starting to work on your foot with their thumb and index finger, easing away any blockages that indicate problems in the corresponding part of your body. Reflexology can be relaxing or energising, depending on what is needed, and the results are instant. Mention to your reflexologist that you have just given up smoking and they will tailor your treatment to help.

TO FIND A REFLEXOLOGIST, CONTACT
The Association of Reflexologists
Tel: 0870 5673320
www.aor.org.uk

FLOTATION

More and more towns have float centres and several health clubs now have their own tanks, so this incredibly powerful therapy is becoming more widely available. Float tanks are soundproofed tanks about 2.5m long and 1.25m wide, containing about 25cm of warm water with plenty of mineral salts dissolved in it so that you can stay afloat in them effortlessly.

You float in complete or semi-darkness, although the door can be left slightly ajar or a light switched on if you prefer. Some float centres play a relaxing sound track at first before you lie in complete silence for approximately an hour.

A therapist will usually talk to you about the experience afterwards, because it can be quite profound, sometimes bringing repressed emotions to the surface. Flotation also stimulates you to produce endorphins, the brain's natural painkillers, and it can stimulate the right side of the brain, promoting creativity. At the very least, you'll feel a deep sense of relaxation after a float session.

TO FIND A FLOAT TANK, CONTACT
The Float Tank Association
Tel: 020 7627 4962
www.floattankassociation.co.uk

HYDROTHERAPY

Find out about the range of water therapies available at your local health club. Water therapies are deeply relaxing, since they generally involve you lying still in warm water which supports the weight of your body.

- Jacuzzis, saunas and Turkish (steam) baths are all quite common now, and are good for eliminating impurities from the system. Try them just after you give up smoking to clear out the nicotine as quickly as possible.

- Thalassotherapy involves the use of jets of seawater or seaweed wraps to cleanse the skin.

- Moor baths have a blend of herbs, which look like muddy sludge in the water. You soak in them for 20 minutes or so.

Alternatively, have a relaxing end-of-the-day routine by creating your own hydrotherapy experience in the bath. Add aromatherapy oils or Epsom salts to the water, play calming music and light candles, then lie back to soothe your troubles away.

Staying
Stopped

THE DANGER ZONE

You've got through the worst of the nicotine withdrawal symptoms and are now officially an ex-smoker, but you're not completely out of the woods. All sorts of challenges lie ahead and the sad truth is that 80% of those who give up will be smoking again within a year. But don't be discouraged.... If you can understand the reasons why other quitters tend to relapse, you're much more likely to be able to rationalise and overcome them yourself when temptation strikes.

Did you choose a quitting plan that was predominantly focused on physical nicotine withdrawal symptoms? If so, you may not have dealt with your psychological addiction. Even if you chose a psychological approach, like hypnotherapy or a course by one of the stop-smoking gurus, the effects can wear off as the weeks roll by. Physical addiction is not terribly hard to overcome, but the mental side can be much tougher, and the problem is that it is your brain you are relying on to keep you a non-smoker.

Danger zones vary from person to person: some can't get through the first 48 hours; others last until the first time they're in the pub with their smoking friends; there's a particular danger zone between six weeks and three months after you stop, when you begin to feel confident and let your guard down; and you will also be at risk if you experience any traumas in the first year or so after you quit and feel the need to turn to your 'old friend'.

One of the hardest phenomena to turn on its head is the feeling of being deprived of a treat, reward or pick-me-up. No matter how much you rationalise that you have given up a habit that was destroying your health and taken a positive, life-enhancing step forwards, there can still be a subconscious feeling of 'Poor me'. The problem is that 'poor me' can easily be translated into 'Life's too short not to be enjoying myself' or 'Just this one, just for now' or 'A quick puff can't do any harm'. When you find yourself thinking this way, sit down, pause and consider the question: do you want to start smoking again? If the answer is no, then don't do it.

All you need to promise yourself is that you will take those few seconds when you are tempted to ask the question: 'Do I want to be a smoker again?' No bargaining, no self-delusion – it's as simple as that. *Do* you want to be a smoker? You've got this far in a book entitled *Stop Smoking*, so somehow I don't think you do.

RELAPSE EXCUSES (AND OTHER SETBACKS)

Read through all the excuses and the rationalisations that follow. Next time one of these or a similar excuse leaps into your brain, with any luck you will remember why it doesn't make any sense.

'I've picked the wrong time to quit. I'm so stressed, I need a cigarette right now.'

Why did you decide in Part 1 that this was a good time to stop? Have circumstances changed since then? Will there ever be a 'right time'? Remember that feeling stressed can be a side effect of nicotine withdrawal and it won't last long if you just hold firm. If you've survived more than 48 hours without smoking, you're past the worst already. It would be crazy to go back and reintroduce nicotine into your brain and bloodstream now, because you would only have to go through the whole process again at a later date. Find some other method of stress relief – there are plenty to choose from in Part 2 – and try to keep going, just a day at a time – or an hour at a time, if need be.

If you can't get through the first 48 hours, even with the techniques you selected from Part 2, then you need some additional help. Reread Parts 1 and 2 and consider the other strategies that would help. A support group? Acupuncture? Homeopathy? Keep trying till you find the one that works for you. You'll get there in the end.

'I quit because my partner wanted me to, but now I just feel furious with him/her, as though they've taken something special away from me.'
It's a mistake to give up smoking for someone else and not for yourself. The resentment it can breed could end up wrecking the relationship. Irrationally, you blame your partner for taking away one of your pleasures in life while they still enjoy all of theirs, be it drinking wine, a weekly massage, a golf game, or whatever they happen to enjoy.

Another possible result could be that it turns you into a 'secret smoker', sneaking the odd fag while out walking the dog, or before your partner gets home from work, then rushing to the bathroom to brush your teeth in a vain attempt to disguise the smell of smoke. If you started smoking as a teenager, you probably tried to hide it from your parents for a while and learned some 'secret smoking' tricks – where to hide the pack and how to get it out of the house without their noticing; perhaps you learned to smoke

TIP: Every year 50 million working days are lost in the UK because of smoking-related illness.

while hanging out of their bathroom window, then sprayed air freshener round the room. Secret smoking is exciting, with all the subterfuge and snatched opportunities making it just like a secret affair, and for this reason it can be harder to give up than out-in-the-open smoking.

If you are worried that you've given up for someone else, stop and consider the benefits that you will reap personally. Think of all the good things that not smoking will bring you and write a list of them. It may help if you try one of the psychology-based techniques, such as hypnotherapy or an Allen Carr course, but do it for yourself this time. Deal with any short-term irrational anger with your partner using oatstraw (see page 128), homeopathic Staphysagria (see page 119) or Bush flower essence Mountain devil (see page 163).

'I haven't had a cigarette for six weeks, so I've successfully given up. Now that I'm in control of smoking, surely it wouldn't hurt to have just one puff?'
During the critical period roughly six weeks to three months after you quit, not smoking no longer feels so difficult. In fact, you're feeling rather confident. Who said quitting smoking was hard? How come 80% of

quitters go back to it within a year? Maybe you've just got stronger willpower than most, you reckon. In which case, your brain argues, surely it would be alright just to have a quick puff every now and then?

There's a golden rule of addiction that your body 'remembers' its optimum level of the substance even years after you give up, and will quickly want to return to it again. For example, imagine an alcoholic who used to drink half a bottle of whisky a day but gave up drinking completely five years ago. One day he thinks to himself, 'After all this time, surely I could risk a little snifter of malt?' Within weeks, or perhaps even days, he would be back on a half bottle of whisky a day again. That's the level his addictive self has settled on and the point he will always return to every time he drinks.

Some experts believe that nicotine addiction is more powerful than cocaine or heroin addiction. If someone had successfully weaned themselves off heroin, gone through cold turkey and come out the other side, do you think it would be a good idea for them to have 'just one little fix'? So what makes you

---

TIP: Smokers can collect a full litre of tar in their lungs in just one year. That's 1¼ pints.

think it's a good idea for you to have just one more puff? Smoking may be more socially 'acceptable', in that you can buy cigarettes from newsagents rather than drug dealers, but it can be even more dangerous for your mental and physical health than hard drugs.

When you hear yourself arguing that just one more puff won't do any harm, remember that it is the first tumble down a very steep and slippery slope back to the 10-, 20-, 40- or 60-a-day habit you had before. Do you want to be a smoker again?

'I just want a quick cigarette to remind myself how disgusting it is, and reinforce my resolve.'
There are plenty of non-addictive ways to remind yourself how foul smoking is. Go into your local pub at closing time and inhale deeply just above one of the overflowing ashtrays; visit an emphysema sufferer in hospital; or just watch the gaunt, pinched faces of smokers you pass in the street, sucking hard on the end of a white paper tube, each of them a drug addict – even if their drug of choice happens to be legal.

Look back at page 78 to remind yourself of the number of cigarettes you have smoked in your life so far. What makes you think that if you smoke one now, it would be the last ever? Doesn't look likely, does it?

In fact, it would more likely be the first of several thousand more to add to your total.

'Some people are just social smokers, only having an occasional cigarette at parties. That's how I would like to be.'

I'm not so sure that those one-at-a-party smokers genuinely exist; if they do, there are very very few of them. Most 'occasional' smokers get through far more cigarettes than they let on to you, or even to themselves. They get withdrawal symptoms the morning after the party and live through them till the next event where they can justify their smoking, and just watch how quickly they top up their nicotine levels once they're there. If they don't have their own pack, they'll make it a priority to ask round the room until they find someone who will give them one, all the while trying to maintain their casual, I-can-take-it-or-leave-it front. They have an addiction that they are feeding sporadically, but over time they will find or invent more and more occasions that can be classed as a 'party'. If their rule is that they only smoke with a drink in their hand, it could mean that they gradually start drinking more to provide the excuse.

You are a step ahead of them because you have accepted that you are addicted to nicotine. Don't forget the rule: 'Once an addict, always an addict.' If you allow yourself that one cigarette at a party, before long you will be back on exactly the same number of cigarettes per day that you used to smoke.

SELF-DECEPTION

If you find yourself indulging in any of the following, you're kidding yourself and will soon be a smoker again:

* Leaning forward to inhale the smoke from friends' cigarettes 'because you like the smell'.
* Lighting friends' cigarettes for them.
* Having a puff on a cigar after a meal 'to see what it tastes like'.
* Having a drag on a friend's pipe, but 'not inhaling'.
* Smoking a marijuana joint that has tobacco in it.
* Holding a cigarette in your fingers, 'just to remind yourself what it feels like'.
* Smoking herbal cigarettes from the chemist (although no one does this for long because they're so foul-tasting and there's no nicotine).

'I've given up cigarettes but I don't seem to be able to wean myself off nicotine replacements.'
It's important that you follow the instructions carefully when using NRTs because while they are not as bad for you as cigarettes, they are still provoking

your adrenaline stress response and putting strain on
your heart and other organs. After using them for the
first few weeks, you will have broken your habitual
smoking pattern but you still have to get the nicotine
out of your system and then let go of the mental
addiction. To cut down on nicotine gum or lozenges,
try substituting every second piece with some
liquorice root (see page 134) or just a stick of sugar-
free gum. Use herbal remedies, homeopathy,
aromatherapy or flower essences to deal with any
physical withdrawal symptoms you experience as you
gradually reduce your NRTs, day by day. Alternatively,
drink a big glass of water or take a full, deep breath
every time you get a nicotine craving, and remember
that they never last longer than three minutes.

By the three-month mark, you should be phasing out
any 'substitutes' you've been using because they will
keep reminding you that you are not smoking and
prevent you from proceeding to the next stage – not
even thinking about smoking. You can spot the ex-
smokers who haven't made this transition because at
every opportunity they talk about how they've given

TIP: As Allen Carr says, 'There is absolutely nothing to give up – there
is no genuine pleasure or crutch in smoking. It is just an illusion, like
banging your head against a wall to make it pleasant when you stop.'

up, they frequently hold forth on what a disgusting habit smoking is, and you see them watch longingly when someone else in the group lights up! Alternatively, every time you look they are chewing manically on a piece of gum, sucking a lozenge, or dragging hard on an inhaler.

When you first give up, it's natural that you are preoccupied by quitting, and it's healthy to keep congratulating yourself on your success. Over the next months, the number of times a day you think about smoking should gradually decrease and cravings should reduce in intensity. This won't happen if you haven't cut out the NRTs; in fact, you are just prolonging the agony.

Don't let 'not smoking' become an obsession. If it does, it may be that you need a psychological therapy, such as hypnotherapy, behaviour modification or a support group or course, to help you move on.

'Why do other smokers seem to want me to fail? One friend in particular still keeps offering me a cigarette every time he has one himself.'
This is simple to answer. Other smokers don't want you to succeed at not smoking because it highlights the fact that they haven't managed it themselves.

They are still hooked on a drug called nicotine and you are not. On the other hand, if you try to stop and fail, it vindicates their excuse that 'It's too hard to give up' or 'You have to wait for the time to be right' or whatever self-deception they are currently using.

They are probably perfectly nice people themselves. I'm sure they're kind to children and animals and drop spare coins into cancer research collecting tins in the street. But that's not going to stop them from 'accidentally' leaving a cigarette burning in the ashtray beside you while they go up to order another round of drinks. And if you have a weak moment and ask them for a puff of their cigarette, you can bet your bottom dollar they'll oblige.

It's even worse if you live with a smoker. They are going to be secretly irritated when you upset the domestic status quo by stopping. Even if they agreed to avoid smoking in the house at first, will they keep it up long term? With the best will in the world, they're bound to leave cigarettes lying around sometimes, so temptation will always be on hand.

It will be best of all if your good example persuades them that it can be done – giving up smoking is possible and desirable and, if you managed it, they should be able to as well. Never try to persuade other smokers to stop. Let them reach their own decision and then, if they ask, give them advice about the methods and techniques that worked for you. Alternatively, suggest that they buy a copy of this book. You could lend them yours, but it will underscore their motivation if they have to go out and buy their own.

If smoking friends continue to try to tempt you back to smoking, you have two options: use their obvious fear and neediness to remind yourself how glad you are that you gave up; or stop seeing them so often so that you don't have to breathe their smoke.

SMOKING DREAMS

Dreaming that you're smoking again after you've stopped is a common phenomenon. It means that you are still thinking about smoking and adjusting to the change, but it doesn't mean that you want to start again. Quite the contrary: usually you are disappointed in yourself in the dream, upset that you're smoking and worried that other people will be disappointed when they find out. It's an enormous relief to wake up and find out that it's not true. These dreams are most common in the first months after you give up, but some ex-smokers report having smoking dreams years after they last lit up.

'I had a few drinks and my willpower went out the window. Before I knew it there was a lit cigarette in my hand and I was smoking it.'

How drunk would you have to be before you put your head down a pub toilet and pulled the flush? Or picked up and ate a piece of dog excrement from the pavement? No matter how drunk we are, most of us still retain enough control of our faculties not to do either of those disgusting things. We can also usually prevent ourselves from having sex with people we don't want to, and most of us remain *compos mentis* enough not to accept lifts with strangers, dive into the nearest river or take severe, unnecessary risks with our personal safety. The point is that alcohol dulls your faculties but it doesn't drown them completely. If you want to say no to smoking, you'll do it – no matter how drunk you are.

This is an example of ways that smokers can sabotage their own attempts to give up (see page 240). Ex-smokers who haven't dealt with their mental addiction can create all kinds of excuses for themselves to relapse, and one of these is getting drunk then saying 'It wasn't my fault. I couldn't help it.' The truth is that you could help it if you wanted to. Take responsibility. Be a grown-up.

If you wake the morning after a drinking binge and realise you smoked the night before, start the Emergency Relapse Plan (see page 233) straight away. If you seem to be binge drinking on a regular basis, see page 247 for advice on whether it is time to take your drinking in hand.

ALCOHOL AND CAFFEINE

After you give up smoking, the effects of alcohol and caffeine can be exaggerated, as your brain and body adjust to the lack of the nicotine stimulus. This means that you can get drunk on fewer drinks than you did before, and more than two cups of coffee might make you jittery or even cause palpitations. Beware of 'substituting' alcohol for cigarettes. Just as many people over-eat when they give up, there are those who increase their alcohol intake, having an extra sip for every drag they would have taken in the past. You could find that you have replaced your nicotine addiction with an alcohol one and have to face a whole new giving-up process (see page 247).

'I've just had a massive bust-up with my partner, I'm shaking with rage, and only a cigarette would calm me down right now.'

Think back to the physiological effects of smoking on the body: adrenaline rush, oxygen deprivation, constricting blood vessels, the lungs becoming coated with tar. How exactly would smoking calm you down? On the contrary, it would fire you up more. Adrenaline is the last thing you need if you are exploding with temper.

After an argument, why not go for some aerobic exercise to burn off your adrenaline and produce the brain's own antidepressant endorphins? After that, find somewhere peaceful to sit down with a pen and a piece of paper and work out what most enraged you about the argument. What most enraged your partner? Often the root cause won't be the same as the immediate trigger. Is your partner right about anything he or she said? Can you think of a constructive way to move towards a resolution? If you can't come up with a solution yourself, is there any wise friend you could discuss it with, who will be even-handed and not take sides automatically?

Storming out to buy a pack of 20 after an argument is such an established stereotype that some ex-smokers who are not really ready to let go of their habit will

TIP: Of course, it's a bad idea to drink too much alcohol at any time, but if you do over-indulge, you'll find that non-smokers' hangovers are much gentler than the kind smokers get.

manufacture an argument from thin air in order to give themselves an excuse to lapse. It's another example of self-sabotage (see page 240). If you're suffering from irritability or aggression as a side effect of nicotine withdrawal, you may be especially likely to choose this course, so get some fast-acting remedies to keep your temper in check: oatstraw (see page 128) or Mountain devil (see page 163) should help.

'I only gave up because I was pregnant. Now I've had the baby, I can't wait to start again.'
If you can't stay off cigarettes for your own sake, can you do it for the sake of your children? No matter how much they fool themselves, no smoking parent entirely manages to protect their children from passive smoking. Think of those soft, pink, vulnerable little lungs getting blackened and losing their elasticity because of your tarry smoke. Think about the fact that your child is likely to be ill more often than his friends who don't have smoking parents, that he will probably do less well at school, and chances are that he will start smoking in his teens, following the example you've set. Re-read pages 26–30 for more ways in which smoking will harm your child.

After you've thought about that, consider the fact that you have got over your physical addiction to

BEREAVEMENT

People who haven't smoked for years can find themselves lighting up at a loved-one's funeral, because they have a vague memory that smoking used to relieve pain and stress and they're grasping at any straws they can think of. The acute, raw pain of a recent bereavement can be so unbearable that it feels as though nothing else matters except finding a way to get through it. But if you're ever in this situation, you must remember that there is no way in which smoking will make things better, not even temporarily. In fact, it will mess with your antidepressant brain chemicals and make things much, much worse.

Your immune system is under a massive amount of stress when you suffer the loss of a loved one, so your resistance to viruses, infections and abnormal, pre-cancerous cells is going to be much lower. This is why it's very important to take care of yourself physically at such times, getting adequate nutrition and plenty of rest. If you start smoking again, you could tip your own balance from health to serious illness. And a few months down the line, you'll have to face the trauma of giving up again. Don't do it to yourself!

nicotine during the last nine months. It would be crazy to reintroduce it to your body unless you have decided categorically that you want to be a smoker for the rest of your life. Do you? Think back to a time before you started smoking. If you had known then all the ways in which it damages your health, causes you stress and misery, wrecks your appearance and turns you into a social outcast, would you have started smoking in the first place? You have that choice now. This is the first day of the rest of your life, and you are at a crossroads. Do you want to live that life as a smoker or as a non-smoker? Decide now.

FATALISM

If you've just been diagnosed with a serious illness, such as cancer, heart disease or lung disease, it's vital that you give up smoking as soon as possible – but many don't manage to. The problem is that you're scared, incredibly stressed, and some people tend towards fatalism, thinking 'The worst has happened. There's no point in giving up now.' But they are so wrong.

Tell your doctor or specialist that you smoke, if they don't know already, and ask their advice. Call the NHS or the Quit helpline for emotional support. See page 197 for advice on how visualisation can help to fight off illness and consider seeing a counsellor or hypnotherapist who can teach you some very effective ways to do this. Don't give up hope. A positive attitude could make all the difference to the outcome of your illness.

'I can't seem to write/paint/design/compose music or be creative any more without a cigarette in my hand.'

Some people buy into this myth that an artist has to suffer to produce great art, that writers are slightly depraved, decadent types and musicians are self-destructive. But it's just that – a myth.

If you were creative before you gave up smoking, you will be creative again once nicotine withdrawal has stopped affecting your concentration and you've got rid of your mental block. In fact, you may find your creativity is enhanced once your brain has completed its detox from all the nasty chemicals you used to introduce to it.

In the meantime, the trick is to sit down and start writing/painting/making music or whatever form of self-expression you enjoy. Just keep going, even if you don't like what's coming out. It won't take long before you re-awaken your creative brain, but you can speed the process by keeping in practice.

TIP: If you're considering re-starting smoking after a period of several months, you are still suffering from mental addiction. Try reading a book, listening to a tape or watching a video by one of the stop-smoking gurus to help you get past the final hurdle.

If you can't shake the idea that smoking was essential to your creativity, try visiting a hypnotherapist or behaviour therapist to break the mental connection. Because it's just not true – it can't be.

'I've put on 10kg and none of my clothes fit any more. I need to smoke again for a while to get my weight down, then I'll give up for good.'
You could spend the rest of your life switching from one addiction to the next unless you break this cycle. You've swapped nicotine addiction for food addiction and now you're considering going back again because of the side effects of food addiction. You're going to have to try something new to break the pattern completely.

Gillian Riley's Full Stop courses (see page 92) specialise in over-eating ex-smokers and, if she doesn't have a course near you, you could benefit from reading her books *How to Stop Smoking, Eating Less* and *Willpower*. A behaviour modification

TIP: You used to enjoy smoking because it relieved nicotine withdrawal symptoms. Once you're past nicotine withdrawal, the 'lapse' cigarette' won't feel the way you remember it. It will make you feel nauseous and dizzy and it will taste disgusting, without giving you the nicotine buzz you used to crave. So why bother?

therapist could help to change your habits in just a few sessions and, if you don't have a fitness programme already, you should join a gym or take up some form of exercise to help you shed the 10kg you've put on. See pages 251-2 for some suggestions.

Don't go on a diet to lose the excess weight. Diets don't work long-term and they create a feeling of deprivation that can make food seem even more desirable. Instead, follow the nutrition advice on pages 138-54 and make sure all the foods that pass your lips are packed with vitamins and minerals. Avoid ready meals and snacks, opt for fresh fruit and vegetables, and the weight should drop off slowly and steadily.

'My marriage just broke up after 15 years and I need a crutch to help me through this period.'
Some smokers find that smoking helps to dull emotional pain and anaesthetise them to an extent in sad situations. Whether there is a physiological reason for this, or it just works because you think it will, is a moot point. Either way it's a bad idea because you are masking your pain rather than attempting to heal it. When you don't face up to strong emotions, they don't disappear; instead, they fester under the surface like an infected wound and it will be much harder to recover fully in the long term.

Everyone should consider some form of counselling after a long-term relationship breaks up, to help them understand what went wrong and how they can avoid making the same mistakes in their next relationship. Maybe your ex-partner will agree to come to Relate with you (tel: 01788 573241 to find your nearest branch). If not, ask your GP to refer you to a counsellor or find one yourself through the British Association of Counselling and Psychotherapy (see page 173).

Take particular care of yourself during the months after the break-up, because your immune system could be compromised (see under Bereavement, page 221). You are at risk of serious illness and smoking is the last thing you should consider.

'I've just been promoted at work and I'm under so much pressure that I could really use a few fag breaks a day to relax.'
Let's unfurl this 'logic'. First of all, far from helping you relax, cigarettes are a stimulant that flood your veins with the stress hormone adrenaline, pushing your heart rate up and making you dizzy and light-headed.

Second, you should be aware that smokers are much less efficient workers than non-smokers. All those fag breaks add up to lower productivity; their nicotine-induced concentration peaks and troughs mean their efficiency is compromised; and they take far more days off sick than non-smokers. Maybe you won't keep that new job for long if you start smoking again.

You need to find some way of dealing with the pressure without resorting to cigarettes. Try one of the following:

- Keep some flower remedies in your desk drawer to dot on your tongue at stressful moments.

- Take a vitamin B supplement daily.

- Install an air ioniser on your desk to revitalise the air by producing streams of energising negative ions.

- Get an executive desk toy to play with, such as clicking balls or magnetic ducks.

TIP: If you are tempted to light up again after a traumatic or sad event, stop and ask yourself logically, 'How will this help?' And you should get the answer that not only won't it help at all, it will actually make things worse because on top of everything else, you'll be a smoker again.

- Install a fish tank and watch the graceful way the brightly coloured fish swim up and down.

- Take up a stress-busting hobby like Yoga, Pilates or T'ai chi. All three of these will teach you some calming movements that can be done at your desk.

- Keep things in perspective. Remember that whatever is stressing you today will probably be resolved tomorrow, and that there are plenty of things in life that are far more important than work.

'I've been so depressed since I gave up smoking and I can't seem to shake it. I'd rather smoke again and be happy than stay this down.'
Depression can be a side effect of giving up smoking, until the brain's dopamine release gets back to normal. It can also result from the erroneous sense that you've been 'forced' to give up something that you used to enjoy. If you're still suffering from depression more than three months after giving up, you should visit your GP and ask for help. He or she may decide to refer you for counselling to uncover the roots of your depression.

For mild to moderate cases of depression, St John's wort (see page 130) is extremely effective, and trials are showing very positive results when it is used by those giving up smoking. You can buy this herbal remedy over the counter in chemists and try it out, so long as you aren't taking any other medication. Allow three weeks for the effects to be noticeable. Homeopaths also have some very effective remedies for depression, which they will tailor according to your individual constitution.

Starting smoking again would be the worst thing you could do, because on top of everything else, you would feel a sense of failure that you didn't manage to quit, and your self-esteem would plummet. See page 252 for more on self-esteem, which is intimately tied up with addictive behaviour.

'I'm on holiday and I want to let my hair down. Surely there wouldn't be any harm in having a couple of cigarettes, in the spirit of self-indulgence. It's not as if I would do it again back home.'
Light one cigarette and you are a smoker again. No matter what excuse you manufacture, you're basically

TIP: If you light up when you're feeling stressed, you not only have to deal with your stress, but you will also have a rapid heart-beat, coughing, a foul taste in your mouth and the horrible knowledge that you have let yourself down.

admitting that you haven't got over your addiction. Say you allow yourself to smoke only when you're on holiday, you might soon be extending the definition of 'holiday' to include weekends away in the country, or reunions with friends you met on holiday, and then you'll start allowing yourself the odd cigarette whenever you want to let your hair down, and before long you'll feel that way 20 times a day.

The problem is that you are still linking smoking in your head with 'pleasure', 'reward', 'relaxation' and 'enjoyment', instead of 'anxiety', 'stress', 'depression' and 'premature death'. Take one of the stop-smoking gurus' books or tapes on holiday with you to read or listen to on the beach or by the swimming pool. They'll enhance your enjoyment of your holiday by reminding you what a wise decision you made when you gave up, and how great it is that you are able to live a happy, smoke-free life now.

'I'm too young to be sensible. Abstinence is boring and straight, and I'd rather be cool and reckless.' Do you want to live hard and die young? Think very carefully about this. What age do you want to die? Next year? The year after? If you started smoking in your teens, you may already have cancer-forming cells in your lung tissue, and lung cancer is not cool.

A type of drug called steroids is one of the treatments, and they quickly make your face swell up like a lumpy potato, while you have to hunch over trying to get enough oxygen into a non-damaged area of your lungs. Leg amputation is not cool either. And you won't be able to hang out at parties any more if you get chronic lung disease.

If you manage to give up in your twenties, there's a good chance you've got away with it. If you don't give up until you are in your thirties, then your health could be permanently damaged. And in your forties and fifties, your smoking-related death is just around the corner. The risk increases with every single cigarette you smoke.

Not smoking is the new cool in the 21st century. It means that you value yourself and think you are worth looking after. In evolutionary terms, you are a giant step ahead of your mouth-breathing smoker friends. Remember the basic law of the universe: it's the fittest who survive.

TIP: Cigarette smoke produces 10 times more air pollution than diesel car fumes. In a confined space, air pollution from smoking can be as much as 15 times that found in the street outside.

There are hundreds more relapse excuses than the ones listed here, because an addict's brain can be an ingenious creature. If you ever hear yourself making one of these excuses, force yourself to stop and remember that there are NO good reasons to start smoking again. Not even one. There are absolutely no benefits from smoking: no situation that it will make easier; no mood that it will improve. Its effects are solely negative: it will deplete your energy, make you more stressed and depressed, and ruin your health.

If you find yourself wrestling with relapse excuses, don't just ignore them. Read back through the Techniques section in Part 2 and choose another tool to help you stay quit. It will be much easier to take pre-emptive action now than to have to give up all over again one day.

TIP: When you get a craving, breathe in through your nose and out through your mouth, blowing the urge to smoke away. Count to 4 on the in-breath and 8 on the out-breath.

THE EMERGENCY RELAPSE PLAN

You wake up in the morning with a stale tobacco taste in your mouth, a throat that feels as though you've swallowed broken glass, a hollow, echoey sensation in your lungs, and a poisonous headache. For some reason, it appears you smoked last night. Don't lie in bed beating yourself up about it, or feeling depressed. Get up immediately and follow the instructions below.

1. Are there any cigarettes left in the house? Check your bag, briefcase, pockets, and the car as well. If you find any, break them into pieces under a running tap and throw them straight into the bin. Empty and clean used ashtrays, and if there are any butts longer than 1cm, break them into pieces and soak them under the tap.

2. Have a shower with the water as hot as you can take it. Wash your hair and use a brush or loofah to scrub your skin. Switch the water to cold and stay under it for two or three minutes to give your circulation a boost.

TIP: Mark Twain once quipped: 'I have no trouble quitting – I've done it a thousand times.' ... Why put yourself through all that grief? Next time you quit, make it forever.

3. Brush your teeth meticulously and swill mouthwash round your mouth.

4. Put the clothes you were wearing in the washing machine, or lay them out to take to the dry cleaners on the way to work.

5. Peel and chop any fruit you have in the house and blend up a fruit smoothie for breakfast. Avoid coffee and toast or cereal. If you must have tea, choose an antioxidant green tea. Take a multi-vitamin and any other supplements you've been taking as part of your quit-smoking attempt.

6. Have a look at your diary for the day and find a space when you can go to the gym, have a swim or a run or play sport. Call a non-smoking friend and ask them to join you.

7. Carry on with whatever you were planning to do with your day, but don't smoke. If there is a social event where you know you will be tempted to smoke, it may be best to drop out.

8. At some point in the day, find half an hour to sit and analyse what made you relapse. You might think it's obvious – 'I got drunk and my mate offered me one' –

but look a bit closer. Why did you get drunk? Had anything stressful or upsetting happened to you during the day? Once you were drunk, why did you over-rule the non-smoking instincts in your rational brain? Are you still secretly missing smoking?

9. Choose another technique or therapy, one that you haven't tried before. This could mean making an appointment with a homeopath, acupuncturist or hypnotherapist; buying a new remedy in your local chemist; reading a book or listening to a tape by one of the stop-smoking gurus. The choice is yours, but try to select something that addresses the trigger that made you relapse. Are you still fighting mental addiction? Have you failed to find a successful method of stress relief? There are plenty to try.

10. Forgive yourself – but don't forgive and forget. Imagine smoking as a deep cavern filled with toxic waste. Dark, sticky, tarry substances, a mysterious grey-white powder and a flickering artificial light are all that is visible at the foot of the cavern. Once you've sunk into it too deeply, there is no way to climb back

---

TIP: Those who say that they 'choose' to smoke are in denial. They're denying the enormous dependence they have on nicotine. There's no such thing as free choice when you're an addict.

out again because the toxins will have infiltrated every cell in your body. Steep slippery walls line the cavern all around, with the odd craggy ledge here and there. At the top, once you lift your head above the precipice, you can see there are blue skies with white lacy clouds, bright sunshine, green grass, a tinkling stream, flowers, and trees. You can smell fresh clean air and feel the breeze on your cheeks.

Last night, you slipped over the edge into the cavern and fortunately you landed on one of the craggy ledges, not too far down. You have been able to clamber out this time and get back into the sunshine. Next time you might fall all the way and never get out again.

TIP: Every time you relapse and return to smoking, you are reinforcing your addiction, and running the risk that you will never be able to stop.

COMMON RELAPSE MISTAKES

Perhaps the most dangerous mistake you can make after you've slipped up and smoked one more cigarette is to think: 'The hell with it! I've started again now, so I might as well buy a pack of 20.' If you manage to limit the damage, nip it in the bud and stop again straight away – for example, after one evening's backsliding – then you don't need to go through the whole giving-up process all over again. You've had a shot or two of nicotine, but not enough for your body to get used to it. It shouldn't be too hard to stop again the next morning, following the Emergency Relapse Plan.

However, if you smoke the next day as well, you've re-established a smoking pattern that you will have to break. The longer you continue to smoke on your relapse, the harder it will be. In other words, the sooner you throw that pack away, the easier it's going to be to regain your ex-smoker status.

Don't give up hope or feel as though you've failed. Every time you relapse, listen to the clues and pick up the information you need to succeed next time. If you feel as though you're stuck and can't see a way forward, consider whether you might be making one of the following common mistakes.

'I KNEW I WOULDN'T MAKE IT'

Some smokers secretly never thought they could manage it, and the relapse confirms their suspicions. If this is your experience, maybe you're privately relieved. Perhaps you think you have an addictive gene, that your nicotine dependence is somehow stronger than anyone else's, that it would be, frankly, impossible for you to manage without cigarettes. This is patently untrue. You survived perfectly well before you ever started smoking and you will be able to again in the future.

Allen Carr finally gave up a 100-a-day habit after several previous attempts, and after 33 years as a confirmed heavy smoker. Countless millions of others have walked away from their smoking habits even though, like you, they didn't think they'd be able to. If you seriously don't think you'll ever be able to give up, try one of the courses like Quit Masters, Gillian Riley's Full Stop or Allen Carr's Easy Way® that offers you repeat visits until you succeed.

• Here's *Financial Times* journalist Sue Norris's report on her visit to Quit Masters: 'I still thought that in just over an hour I'd be over the road having a quick smoke outside the tube station before stomping home in a temper. I'm not sure how it happened …

but I have not had a cigarette since. ... Weirder still, I have not wanted a cigarette; nor do cigarettes bother me. I seem to have stopped thinking about them.'

- Here's what Allen Carr says: 'I have still not met anybody who was as badly hooked (or, rather, *thought* he was as badly hooked) as myself. Anybody can not only stop smoking but find it easy to stop.'

- Here's a satisfied Full Stop client: 'Although I wanted to stop, I had severe doubts that I could. When I started the course I was on about thirty a day... I realised I had completely lost control over my smoking. During the course, because of my misgivings, I think I was unconsciously resisting the technique. I frequently felt cross and couldn't believe it could possibly work... A year on I feel quite secure around cigarettes and other smokers. They don't bother me. I don't feel I want to boast that I've stopped smoking; I just accept and am glad that it has happened.'

These courses cost money – a couple of hundred pounds or more – but calculate how quickly you will have made a profit when you are saving all that money not buying cigarettes. Check the chart on page 75. A pack-a-day smoker could be in profit after six weeks of not smoking. If you don't have the money to pay for one of these courses, try the free NHS clinics or support groups in your area, use the Quit free telephone and e-mail advice lines, or consider joining Nicotine Anonymous if you live in the south-east of England.

SELF-SABOTAGE

Fear is one of the reasons that drives people to sabotage their own attempts to quit – fear that it is going to be too difficult and you won't manage it anyway, so why bother? The other cause is low self-esteem. Surprised? Maybe you don't think of yourself as having low self-esteem: you could be a high-flyer at work, hugely popular in your circle of friends, and the life and soul of every party. Yet, if you are still smoking and unable to quit then you have an internal voice whispering to you that you're not strong enough, you don't deserve to have good health, that you're not worth the effort.

People with high self-esteem look after themselves and, if the going gets tough, they persist. Those with low self-esteem might go through the motions but they trip at the first hurdle – or they get so anxious that they actually create their own hurdle to fall at.

All kinds of people sabotage themselves as they approach the height of their success: sportspeople who've made it to the semi-finals of a competition suddenly sustain an injury that prevents them getting through to the final; actors reading for a big film role fluff their lines; an architect submitting a plan for an international commission misses the final closing date for entries.

There are many variations on this theme, but in each case it occurs because subconsciously they can't see themselves as a winner. Deep inside, they feel they don't deserve to win; they get anxious as potential success beckons and so they sabotage it.

One solution might be to go into therapy and find out why you don't have healthy self-esteem. Alternatively, in the case of smoking, you just need to grit your teeth and keep going, over-ruling your inner voices and saboteur instincts. Keep trying positive visualisations. After you haven't been smoking for a while, you'll find that the fear disappears and your self-esteem automatically lifts.

TIP: Smoking filtered, lower-tar cigarettes does not reduce the risk of coronary heart disease, but it can make you vulnerable to a particular kind of cancer of the lungs, called adenocarcinoma.

Your self-image will change once you are a successful non-smoker. You have achieved something very important, taken responsibility for your own health and passed the challenge. See pages 252-3 for some ways you can capitalise on the surge of self-esteem that can follow in the wake of giving up smoking. The better you feel about yourself, the less likely it is that you will ever backslide again.

YO-YO QUITTERS

If you get into a cycle of repeated relapsing and having to give up again, you may need some additional help to stop the yo-yo effect.

Are you relapsing for the same reasons every time? If so, select another technique from Part 2 and see if it makes the difference. None of the techniques work for everyone. Quitting smoking is an individual process with no one-size-fits-all solution. Some people respond to homeopathy and others don't, but those who don't might well find that acupuncture is the answer. Combine a physical and a psychological therapy of your choice to maximise your chances.

TIP: Don't bank on getting a clear early warning sign that smoking is damaging your health. The first-ever smoking-related symptom you get could be a fatal heart attack.

If you don't worry too much about relapsing because you find it relatively easy to give up, you should be aware that you are fooling yourself. You may feel smug that you don't suffer debilitating nicotine withdrawal symptoms, as other people do, but you have never managed the really tricky bit, which is overcoming mental addiction. You are still a smoker, even if you haven't had a cigarette for a week or two. Because you haven't genuinely given up, you never move into the next stage, when you know that you can relax because you have conquered smoking once and for all.

Think about the fact that your cells are constantly having to adapt and re-adapt to the changing circumstances. One day they are fighting off tars and toxins; next day they are not, so they start to clean out and detox, then along come more tars and toxins. Be aware that cancers take root when cells are in a process of change, and yours are being forced to change fairly regularly.

If you are a yo-yo quitter who finds it easy to give up, you need to take yourself in hand psychologically or you will continue this way for the rest of your life. Read one of the stop-smoking gurus' books, or listen to a tape; make an appointment with a hypnotherapist or a behaviour therapist. Admit that you are an addict, even if you are only feeding the addiction sometimes and not all the time. Knock your habit on the head, once and for all.

WHEN CAN YOU RELAX?

How will you know when you've finally cracked it? Obviously, time is the true test, but every time you get through a situation that would previously have had you reaching for the fags, you are getting stronger.

If you go on holiday and don't consider smoking in that pretty bar overlooking the bay when there's a beer at your elbow, you're doing fine. If you lose your job, or your partner, or if someone close to you dies and you don't beg a cigarette from the nearest smoker, you can be pretty sure that you're cured. After a year or so, you'll hardly think about smoking any more, even when others are smoking around you – and that's a good way to be.

From time to time you might get a flashback, and it's usually to the nicotine buzz, that moment when you

---

TIP: Sixty percent of the adult population have been addicted to nicotine at one time; only 25% are now. That means that 35% have successfully given up.

take a first drag and the brain stimulates the release of adrenaline. Allow yourself to remember that feeling of inhaling smoke deep into your lungs. When you are genuinely free of the influence of cigarettes, you will be able to relive the memory of that buzz, but it will no longer be tempting you to smoke because your brain will be quietly reminding you of all the downsides as well.

Allen Carr claims that when he came up with his 'method', he immediately knew that he would never smoke again, and he invites you to feel the same way. Most smokers don't have a blinding epiphany moment like this; instead, there's a gradual, growing awareness that you've made it this time. And it's a very good feeling.

TIP: Nothing can be so bad that a cigarette won't make it worse. Feeling stressed? Nicotine would wind you up more. Feeling sad? Cigarettes have a depressant effect.

PASSIVE SMOKING

Researchers are finding that passive smoking is much more dangerous than it was ever thought to be. The non-smoker who is in the same room as a smoker is breathing sidestream smoke from the burning tip of the cigarette and mainstream smoke that the smoker has exhaled. Just 30 minutes' exposure to other people's smoke will reduce the coronary blood flow in a non-smoker.

Over the longer term, passive smokers' risk of serious and fatal diseases is substantially increased; for example, they have a 25% greater chance of getting heart disease or lung cancer than non-smokers. Professor Konrad Janrozik of Imperial College, London, estimates that in the UK passive smoking causes 3,600 deaths a year amongst those who live with a smoker and 700 deaths a year among those who work in a smoky atmosphere.

After you've given up smoking, you may begin to share non-smokers' concerns about passive smoking and do your best to avoid other people's smoke. In opinion polls, 86% of the public (including smokers) agreed that smoking should be restricted in the workplace and in restaurants. If you agree that the UK government should ban smoking in public places, as has been successfully done in Ireland, New Zealand, California and New York, then write to your MP.

BECAUSE YOU'RE WORTH IT

Most people give up smoking because they want to enjoy good health for as long as they can, and cut their risk of serious illness. Once you've dumped your smoking habit and are getting plenty of energising oxygen into your bloodstream again, why not address a few other areas of life to capitalise on the health benefits?

Don't rush to do everything straight away, or even within the first three months after you quit, because not smoking will require your focused attention for a while. You have taken a huge step towards changing your mindset and prioritising your own wellbeing. You will already be feeling the effects on your health and fitness and also on your self-esteem.

If you look after your body, it will continue to look after you in return, keeping you younger-looking and more active than your less healthy contemporaries. Consider whether it would be helpful for you to address any of the following issues next.

How much alcohol do you drink?

More than 14 units a week if you're a woman, or 21 units if you're a man? A unit is a half pint of beer, a small glass of wine or one measure of spirit. If you regularly drink more than this, or if you binge drink 6 or more units in one session, then you are putting your health at serious risk. One in three heavy drinkers dies of heart attacks in middle age, and one study puts the average age of death at 52.

You don't have to be 'an alcoholic' for your health to suffer (and different experts and groups define that term in different ways). The truth is that if you regularly resolve to try and cut down on the amount you drink, or if you feel you need alcohol to relax and have fun, then you have a problem. Try reading Allen Carr's book *The Easy Way to Control Alcohol*, or Bert Pluymen's *The Thinking Person's Guide to Sobriety*.

If you know you have a drinking problem, call Alcoholics Anonymous (tel: 0845 7697555) to find the location of your nearest meeting and go along. You'll find them incredibly welcoming and helpful.

Do you take street drugs?

It's unlikely that you found the motivation to give up smoking if you are still taking illegal drugs such as ecstasy, cocaine, speed, crack or heroin – but if you are, you know you have to take yourself in hand. There's plenty of help out there. Start by talking to your GP or call Narcotics Anonymous (tel: 020 7730 0009).

What about legal drugs?

Do you rush for paracetamol or aspirin every time you have a mild headache? Paracetamol challenges your liver and aspirin can cause stomach ulcers; a cup of chamomile tea or some lavender aromatherapy oil would be much gentler alternatives. Do you expect your doctor to prescribe antibiotics every time you catch a cold? You could be making yourself resistant so they won't work any more when you really need them.

Allopathic medicine, as prescribed on the NHS, is generally effective at treating acute problems but less successful with long-term, chronic, niggling aches and pains or recurrent infections. If you suffer from stiff, painful joints, a glucosamine supplement can be more effective than the non-steroidal anti-inflammatory drugs your doctor might prescribe. Herbal supplements and lifestyle changes can help to lower high blood pressure more effectively than beta-blockers. Evening primrose oil has long been accepted as a treatment for PMS and is much better for you than hormone supplements.

TIP: Don't self-prescribe more than one remedy at a time, and don't take them if you are on any other medication. Consult a qualified practitioner who is registered with the discipline's main regulatory body.

Speak to your acupuncturist, herbalist or homeopath about any non-acute health problems and you may find that they have a safe and effective solution to suggest.

How safe is your food?

Watch out for nasty hidden ingredients in processed foods, such as E numbers and trans-hydrogenated fats. Buy organic meats and fish to avoid the drugs routinely administered to battery-farmed animals and choose organic fruits and vegetables to avoid the pesticides used on non-organic produce.

You will maximise your chances of good health if you stick to the nutritional advice given on pages 138-54 long after you've quit your smoking habit. There are no complex figures to count or calculations to make. Simply eat your food in as fresh, natural and unprocessed a state as possible, keep your diet varied, and make sure everything you eat or drink has nutritional benefits.

Do you need to detox?

Some complementary therapists recommend that you do a detox once a year to cleanse your liver, kidneys and digestive system. There are a number of detox diet books on the market, but Carol

Vorderman's are popular because they feature tasty, easy-to-prepare meals that don't leave you hungry.

While you are detoxing, avoid alcohol, caffeine, wheat, meat and dairy produce. Some vitamin and mineral supplements may be recommended, and you can choose herbs such as milk thistle to speed the detox process. Dry-brush your skin before showers to help release toxins trapped in the tissues and break down cellulite deposits. You'll lose weight, tone up and glow with health after a detox.

How often do you exercise?

You should try to get some exercise every day, alternating aerobic sessions that give you a heart and lung workout with anaerobic exercises that improve muscle tone and flexibility. So, for example, you might do a run in the park one day and a T'ai chi class the next; or swimming then Pilates; or cycling then yoga. If you are a member of a gym, get an instructor to give you an induction and work out some balanced routines for you, using the gym equipment.

On days when you can't slot in time for exercise, try to do some power walking on the way to the shops or the office, climb stairs rather than taking the lift, or do the housework as energetically as you can.

Keep a note of the distances you can cover, your speeds, or the number of repetitions of exercises you achieve, so you can chart your progress over the weeks. If you keep up a routine, you will see and feel improvements almost every week.

TYPES OF EXERCISE	
Aerobic	**Anaerobic**
Running	Weight lifting
Swimming	Body toning classes
Boxing	T'ai chi
Dancing	Pilates
Skiing	Stretching
Ball sports	Yoga
Cycling	Spot exercises

How is your mental health?

Giving up smoking is a huge step towards increasing your self-esteem. If you want to continue building your mental wellbeing, try setting and achieving goals in other areas of your life. Every few months, take some time to assess your relationships, your home life, social life, work life and leisure time. Which areas do you want to improve? What would make things better? And how can you do it? Write a journal in which you list your goals and chart your progress towards them.

Human beings are imaginative creatures and everyone should have a creative outlet of some kind, whether it is gardening, cooking, playing an instrument, writing poetry, painting landscapes, making clay pots or designing your own clothes. Finding creative satisfaction is especially important for ex-addicts who used their addictions to mask an empty feeling inside. Some may also discover that religion, or their own brand of spirituality, helps to answer that nagging 'What's it all about?' feeling. Alternatively, voluntary work for a charity that interests you could open up a whole new perspective on the world.

Keep questioning, being open to new experiences and moving forwards. Make sure that every year you introduce some new element into your life. Don't stop evolving!

If you create an all-round healthy lifestyle, your self-image will change for the better. As your self-respect grows, those around you will also begin to respect you more. It's a positive cycle that only gets better. It would be unthinkable to light a cigarette after a day of high quality nutrition, fresh air and exercise. Once you've experienced all the benefits of a healthy lifestyle for yourself, there really is no going back.

TEN THINGS YOU CAN DO NOW YOU'RE AN EX-SMOKER

1. Play the trumpet, saxophone, flute, clarinet, tuba – even the bagpipes.

2. Walk up hills and hold a conversation at the same time, rather than going red in the face and panting.

3. Get cheaper life insurance, health insurance and mortgage deals. It's very satisfying ticking the non-smoker box on official forms.

4. Kiss your lover first thing in the morning without worrying about having revolting breath. (And have a more fulfilling sex life.)

5. Enjoy theatre, concerts, opera and dance performances and chat to friends during the interval without having to nip outside for a smoke.

6. Achieve great things because your brain will function more efficiently now it's getting more oxygen.

7. Feel in control of your life, without any guilt, fear or dependency.

8. Extend your social circle and visit new friends' homes or new restaurants without worrying about whether it's OK to smoke there.

9. Smell subtle scents like wet gorse, fresh rosemary, newly dug earth and your child's hair.

10. Live a longer, healthier, happier life.

CONTACT US

If you manage to give up smoking using a method that's not described in this book, that other smokers could benefit from, please write to us at the postal or e-mail address below. Your advice could be useful in a future edition.

Editorial Dept
Text Reference
HarperCollins Publishers
Westerhill Rd
Bishopbriggs
Glasgow G64 2QT

E-mail: textreference@harpercollins.co.uk

ACKNOWLEDGMENTS

Grateful thanks to the following for their advice and help (although the views expressed in this book do not necessarily reflect theirs).

Gloria May, hypnotherapist
Tel: 020 7486 4553
E-mail: gloria.may@chilternstreet.co.uk

Eve Rogans, acupuncturist
Tel: 020 7813 3708

Melanie Woollcombe, homeopath
Tel: 020 7693 2267

Sue Reid Sexton, counsellor
Tel: 0141 422 1472
www.suereid.co.uk

Quit Masters UK
Tel: 0800 298 5155

Nicotine Anonymous
Tel: 020 7976 0076
www.nicotine-anonymous.org

Karen Sullivan, expert on nutrition, flower remedies and child care
www.youroverweightchild.org

Action on Smoking and Health
Tel: 0800 169 0169
www.ash.org.uk

Quit
Tel: 0800 002200
E-mail: info@quit.org.uk
www.quit.org.uk